A Darkness of Her Own

Living With the Consequences of Medical Malpractice

Kenneth Zarecor

iUniverse, Inc.
New York   Bloomington

A Darkness of Her Own
Living With the Consequences of Medical Malpractice

*This is a true story. All names, except those of the author and his immediate
family, have been changed. The quotations from the trial and the examinations
before trial were taken verbatim from the official transcripts of those
proceedings. Some of this testimony was edited for the sake of brevity; in
such cases the only change to the testimony is that it was shortened.*

iUniverse books may be ordered through booksellers or by contacting:

iUniverse
1663 Liberty Drive
Bloomington, IN 47403
www.iuniverse.com
1-800-Authors (1-800-288-4677)

*Because of the dynamic nature of the Internet, any Web addresses or links contained in
this book may have changed since publication and may no longer be valid. The views
expressed in this work are solely those of the author and do not necessarily reflect the
views of the publisher, and the publisher hereby disclaims any responsibility for them.*

ISBN: 978-1-4502-3402-3 (sc)
ISBN: 978-1-4502-3403-0 (dj)
ISBN: 978-1-4502-3404-7 (ebook)

Library of Congress Control Number: 2010909152

Printed in the United States of America

iUniverse rev. date: 06/15/2010

Dedicated to Linda and her crew—Dan, Brenda, Ty, Jim, Carrie, Miranda, and Riley—the very best on a daily basis.

ONE

A love of opera brought us together. But the catalyst for our meeting was a wild-haired woman waiting on line in the lobby of the new Metropolitan Opera just after it opened in the fall of 1966.

I'd just recently returned to the United States in the spring of that year after sixteen months in England, where I'd gone to opera, theater, and concerts. In England, I had also indulged a recurring fantasy of mine—to study singing.

I was very excited to get in to see the new theater. The problem was when it opened, there were no tickets of any kind available for several weeks. That was until, according to an opera-fanatic friend, some SRO—standing room only—tickets became available for performances of *La Traviata*. It took some doing, but I convinced my boss at the Port Authority Bus Terminal to let me extend my thirty-minute lunch break to go to Lincoln Center.

It was a crisp early autumn day in New York, and I rushed uptown on the subway and dashed into the Met's sparkling new home. There were several lines on both sides of the lobby, but no clear indication of what was being sold at any of the windows. I didn't have all day, so I just looked for the shortest line. Thinking I'd hit the jackpot, I found a line that consisted of just two people—a man at the window and a woman on line—on the left side of the lobby. I quickly jumped in that line.

The man at the window was standing on tiptoe, trying to hold onto the ledge with one hand while waving the other hand in the air. Even on tiptoe, he could barely see into the ticket cage, and he kept bumping his head as he moved around trying to adjust his position. The wild hand movements, along

1

with the constant adjustments to his feet, made it appear as though he were doing a dance to the sound of his own voice.

The woman wore glasses that appeared to be at least two inches thick. She kept running one hand through her hair, changing the shape of her hairdo, but doing nothing to tame the large clumps of hair that reappeared as quickly as her hand left her head. In her other hand, she held several sheets of paper, which she kept shuffling around, making a clucking sound with each shuffle. As I waited I snuck a peek at the papers: they were all headed, "TENTATIVE CASTING: METROPOLITAN OPERA, 1967–68 SEASON."

My first inclination was to ask her where she'd gotten the casting lists, and if they were real. But instead I only asked, "Is this the line for tickets?"

"I certainly hope so," she laughed, not looking up. "That's why I'm here."

I glanced at my watch, then back at the window. The man behind the window was making motions as though he were throwing a football. It seemed a little odd. Neither he nor the man on tiptoe seemed to be holding tickets. And there was no sign above the cage to indicate what kinds of transactions took place there.

"How long have you been here?" I nervously asked the woman.

"All my life," she replied, again not looking up from her papers. "I was born here."

"What?" I said. "No. I don't mean in New York, I mean on this line."

"A while already," she replied. "In fact, too long."

I glanced again at my watch, and she finally stopped riffling through the sheets of paper.

"That midget," she said, nodding toward the ticket window and speaking in a voice loud enough to be heard throughout the lobby, "has been talking to the ticket man all this time and not one ticket has passed between them. Why don't you go see what those lines on the other side of the lobby are for?"

Her loud comments caused the man behind the window to look up and glare at her. She glared right back at him. "I can tell you right now, Letty," the ticket man hissed, "this line is for subscription returns. The standing room tickets, for you poor slobs that have to stand, are sold on the other side."

I was still new enough to New York City to find this kind of rudeness and confrontation surprising. I hadn't quite figured out how to respond. I only knew that my extended lunch break was nearly over, and I still wasn't even on the right ticket line.

"The midget's name is Donnie," Letty said, taking my arm and leading me across the lobby. "We fight all the time."

She steered me through the large crowd, all the time yelling over her shoulder. "Why don't you get a box to stand on?" she shouted. "You won't have to keep hitting your mouth on the counter." A few people glanced up, but most of the jaded New Yorkers simply ignored the whole scene. "If you keep hitting your mouth on the counter, Donnie, you'll lose all your new false teeth." Letty continued, as though she were addressing a large audience. "He thinks Corelli is the greatest tenor since Caruso. I think his brain stopped growing even before his body did."

Letty let go of my arm when we came to the ticket windows on the right-hand side of the lobby. "Well, look who's here!" she exclaimed, pointing in the general direction of one of the lines. I couldn't see clearly to whom she was talking. "So what are you guys here to buy?"

"Hi, Letty," came a cluster of female voices.

"We heard you fighting with Donnie—again," one female voice said.

"More like still fighting with him," said another voice.

"That *shmegegge*," Letty said, speaking in the direction of the voices, "is always a pain in the *tuches*."

"*Shmegegge?*" exclaimed yet another voice. "*Tuches?* Wow, what kind of a vocabulary is that for a good Catholic girl? The nuns would be horrified!" Several people in the line laughed.

I could now make out that Letty was talking to a group of three women near the end of one of the lines. "So what are you here to buy?" Letty repeated impatiently.

The discussion of the appropriate Yiddish curse for Donnie was not, however, concluded. Another of the women said, "And he's not a *shmegegge*, you know—more like a *shmendrick*. He's more of a weasel or pipsqueak. *Shmegegge* is too mean a word for him, the poor *schlemiel*. Although, since this is a cultured crowd and mixed company, I guess we should be glad you didn't call him a *schmuck!*" This speaker had a mass of dark hair and also a fairly massive amount of weight on her body.

Finally getting to Letty's question, one of the women said, "I'm just here with Raven." She was an attractive blonde with smiling blue eyes.

"So am I," added the heavyset woman. "And she's here—"

"She's here," interrupted the third woman, "to beg, borrow, or scrounge two seats to a *Frau*." This must be Raven. She was petite and had dark eyes, which she held in a calm, steady gaze as she looked at the two of us. Of the three women, Raven was certainly the one that caught second looks. "Maybe you can help me, Letty?"

Maybe I can help with a standing room ticket," Letty said, "but I bet you are looking for a sitting-down ticket, right?"

"*Frau?*" I asked, somewhat incredulously. "You are talking about *Die Frau ohne Schatten?* That's sold out, too?"

"*Frau* is the one real hit of the new season in the new house," the blonde told me. "Don't tell me you don't like Strauss!"

"*Oy vey,*" Letty said. "If I can use an Irish expression my Italian mother always used, I've led this poor Daniel into the lion's den."

"Your name is Daniel?" the heavy girl asked me. "I love Biblical names. Can I call you Dan?"

"You can call me Dan," I replied, "but my real name is Kenneth."

The large woman's eyes narrowed. She inclined her head and leaned toward me. She almost whispered as she spoke. "Then why did she call you Daniel?"

I started to answer, but the blonde interrupted. "You're asking for a lot of frustration to even try to explain it," she said, also speaking in a near whisper. She extended her hand and gave a little laugh. "Hello, Kenny. My name is Lorraine. Even if you don't like Strauss, you should see this production. It really is magnificent. And don't worry about Manya." Lorraine nodded toward the heavy woman. "The music she hears is uniquely her own."

"My name is Manya," the large woman said, confirming what Lorraine had said, and taking my hand out of Lorraine's.

"And I'm Raven, which you've probably figured out." Raven didn't offer her hand, so Manya kept holding onto mine. "And you've already met Letty. How'd you meet her? And what are you here to buy?"

Before I could say anything, Letty answered for me. "He was on the other side, waiting with me for tickets."

"Obviously he works fast, Letty," Manya said, wagging a finger at both of us. "He had you by the arm when you came around the corner."

"I am a person looking for a ticket to the opera," I said warily to the four women. "A cheap ticket to the opera. And I have to be back at work five minutes ago."

"What's that accent?" Raven asked. "You're obviously not from New York. Are you British?"

"That accent is southern," Lorraine said, shaking her head in certainty, obviously confident she was correct, "not British."

"That's interesting," I said, "because I'm neither British nor southern. I'm from Nebraska."

"Nebraska!" Lorraine exclaimed. "Nobody—but nooobody—is from Nebraska! I always thought Nebraska was an invention of Willa Cather."

"Look, Lorraine," Letty said as she put a hand on Lorraine's shoulder, "if your mother can be from Kiev, why can't Kenneth here come from Nebraska?"

"Wow!" Manya said. "I guess somebody has to come from there. Isn't that so, Kenneth? And if you can be strange and bred well, you can be strange and bred well from Nebraska. You look like you're bred well. Even if you are not, if somebody didn't come from there, there wouldn't be anyone there, would there? And if everyone comes from there, there also wouldn't be anyone there anymore, would there?"

The other three women nodded as if in agreement, or as if what Manya had just said made any sense. It was clear to me that this woman was truly listening to her own music. The thought also came to mind that perhaps I should have stayed at work and worried about an opera ticket another time.

"You girls are mean," Raven laughed. "Look, Kenneth, if you'll take it, I have a standing room ticket for tonight's *Traviata*. It only costs a dollar-fifty."

"Only a dollar-fifty to hear Anna Moffo wobble from octave to octave," Manya said through gritted teeth. "And to hear Bruno Prevedi desperately seek any true pitch."

"Come on, Raven," Lorraine said. "Maybe he doesn't even like Moffo. She is a great-looking *Violetta*, but that voice is shot to hell by now. Maybe he doesn't even like her."

"I've only heard her on records and broadcasts," I said.

"Well, the real problem is with Prevedi—the tenor," Letty chimed in, again assuming a voice that could be heard throughout the lobby, and maybe even in the rest of the Lincoln Center campus. "Another great voice with a two-year career."

"Wait, wait," I interrupted Manya before she could weigh in. "I heard him in London at Covent Garden. He was great. Maybe the house is just too big for him?"

"No, no," Manya said with the other women shaking their heads in agreement. "You can sing Alfredo in any size house, with any size voice, if you know what you're doing. I don't know what his problem is, but this man just isn't living up to his promise."

"Well, Raven, whatever," I said, glancing again at my watch for the millionth time. "Can I buy the ticket? I have to get back to work."

"Where do you work?" Lorraine asked.

"I work for Greyhound," I said, exchanging the money for the ticket with Raven.

After a quick, "Good-bye, ladies, it was nice to meet you," I pocketed the ticket and ran for the subway, arriving back at work only five minutes late. That night, as I took my place in the Family Circle Standing Room section, Lorraine, Raven, and Manya greeted me.

TWO

It wasn't a complete surprise to see the three women. Raven had called me at work. The call was a surprise because, although I had mentioned the name of my employer, I hadn't told them the location of my job, and Greyhound had a large operation in New York at that time. Raven called to ask if I wanted to have a hamburger with the "bunch" before the performance.

I couldn't join them because I had to work, but the call lent the rest of the afternoon a pleasant anticipation. Raven attracted the attention of men wherever she went. It wasn't just the dark, silky hair, or the clear, glowing skin. She had a way of looking directly at you while conversing, giving you the impression that you held her total, undivided attention. For a long time, whenever I thought of Raven, the lines written by Lord Byron came to mind:

She walks in beauty, like the night
Of cloudless climes and starry skies.

The other two women were interesting, too. Lorraine was cheerful, optimistic, and she laughed easily. Manya was also always good for a laugh, even though it usually came from her nonstop misquotation of famous lines. If nothing else, Manya's conversation was like a crossword puzzle or parlor game. The listener always had to try to figure out what the accurate version of the quotation was.

Raven was the first to greet me, extending her hand when I reached the Family Circle at the top of the Met. "We came to see how you'd stand up under a truly mediocre night at the opera," she said. "Too bad you had to miss supper and face this cast on an empty stomach."

"Yes," agreed Manya, who also shook my hand. "Still, the music is nice. As Richard Wagner said, 'It's amazing how entertaining cheap music can be.'"

Lorraine stepped forward and kissed me on the cheek. "Wagner nor anyone else in the world ever said that. Or anything close to it."

"Maybe she is thinking of the Noel Coward line," I said. "I think he said something like 'Extraordinary how potent cheap music is.'"

"See?" Lorraine nudged Raven. "He doesn't have an English accent at all. He doesn't pronounce 'extraordinary' in the proper English way."

As the lights dimmed, the two of them competed in a pronunciation contest.

Lorraine stood beside me during the first act, discussing her job as a medical secretary. Manya served this duty during the second intermission, discussing the performances of *Hamlet* I'd seen at Stratford-upon-Avon. "I love that whole 'This is not to be, that is the question' speech and all the other speeches," she told me. I made one attempt to correct the quotation but could not.

The logical progression would have had Raven as my standing companion for the third act, but it turned out all three women left after the second act. Instead of the lovely Raven, I got to stand next to Donnie, the guy Letty had insulted earlier in the day.

"You want to see *Frau* next week?" he asked me as he took his place beside me just as the third act was starting. "I have a ticket for you, if you do."

"What?" I exclaimed as I took the ticket. "How—"

"Don't bother to pay me," Donnie told me. "Letty gave it to Manya to give to you in any case. Manya gave it to Lorraine. She gave it to me to give to you."

"Why didn't Lorraine or Manya just give it to me?"

"Who? Letty? She hates the soprano. She's not even here tonight, I think. Lorraine couldn't find you. Manya forgot until she was running out," Donnie explained as if it all made perfect sense. "It all works out, I guess," he said with a shrug, and then changed the subject.

After the music started, Donnie, as he did at every performance I ever saw him attend, went to sleep. And snored. His was a low-pitched snoring with a kind of a humming sound.

Lorraine called me on Friday afternoon of that same week to ask if I knew about the line for standing room tickets. She explained that the standing room tickets were sold every Sunday at noon, but to make certain they got the best available tickets, buyers joined a list that started on Friday afternoons. Without many other options to get a ticket, I stopped by on my way home from work to add my name to the SR list.

As it turns out, Manya controlled the list. The line was in the large plaza at Lincoln Center. Manya interrupted a conversation in Italian with an older couple to introduce me. "Laura and Vinnie," she said, pointing to me, "I want you to meet Kenneth, who's from Kansas. No, not Kansas. Don't tell me, Kenny—Idaho? No, that's not it either. Wyoming? Yes—maybe not—it's Wyoming, right? No, I got it—Nebraska!" she exclaimed. "Yeah—I got it, Nebraska! I usually do get things correct the first time!"

"You'd think you were from Outer Mongolia or something," Laura said, taking my hand.

Vinnie just shook his head and laughed. "Manya," he said to her, "*Sei pazza nel testa.*" Then he looked at me and added, "Don't mind Manya. She can only remember places next to Zabar's or Lincoln Center." We all, including Manya, laughed. "So, you like the new house?"

"Well," I said, "I've only been in once, to see the *Traviata*. The house is a little too red, but the acoustics are very good which is, I guess, the most important thing about an opera house."

"Yes, the acoustics are great," Laura said. "Too bad you had to see the Met at its most mediocre."

"Robert Merrill was in good voice, and he is the best baritone in the world in his part," Manya interjected. *"Ma il tenore non canta bene, e la diva, come si dice in italiano, peccato, peccato ..."*

"Wait, Manya," Laura laughed. "Maybe Ken doesn't speak Italian."

"I speak enough to know that 'the tenor doesn't sing well, and, as one says in Italian, about the soprano, too bad, too bad ...'"

I became a regular on the line for standing room tickets and got to know Manya, Lorraine, and Raven there and at performances. My relationship with the three women was, at first, casual. I'll admit I was trying to get the attention of Raven. However, she was looking for a medical man, preferably a surgeon. Since Raven was in her thirties, even a dentist would be considered. Manya, in one of her more snide moods, said, "Raven is far enough into her thirties to see the next 'zero' comin' round the corner. Maybe, for her, forty is only a matter of weeks or months away." Manya laughed and continued. "You know, what this really means is that if she finds a 'medical man' to marry her, it will be an *alter cocker*. Just what every girl dreams of: marrying an old fart that she will have to take care of her whole married life."

There was never much of a chance for a serious relationship with Manya, primarily because of her physical size, but also because of her manic depressive behavior. At times, she would chatter away, getting louder and louder, freely misquoting everything that was ever spoken or written. Then, sometimes in midsentence, she would withdraw and would not respond to word or touch.

It was with Lorraine that I had the most contact and the easiest relationship.

Through the first several months of knowing each other, all four of us would meet for a meal and then go to a performance, usually at the Met. Eventually, however, I noticed that Manya and Raven would find some excuse to leave Lorraine and me alone after a performance. At first, I thought this was because I had never indicated any interest in Manya other than as a theater companion, and Raven had made it clear that I was "professionally unsuitable" to her mother.

I realized another consideration was at work when Raven called me and asked if I would take her to a concert at a church on the East Side of Manhattan. "I just can't go alone," she said. "It's an important social event for my job."

I started to make a joke about my "professional unsuitability" when she added, "I hope you can go with me, but be sure it's all right with Lorraine before you answer 'yes.'"

THREE

I started to ask Raven why Lorraine would care if I spent an evening with her, but it suddenly occurred to me what the answer to that question would be. Lorraine and I were spending a lot of time together. We couldn't have come from more different backgrounds, and our conversations revealed a whole new world to me.

She had lived her whole life in New York City, mostly in Brooklyn. Her father, she told me, had died when she and her only brother, Lenny, were small children. Until her mother remarried, Lorraine spent most of her time pretending to be the daughter of an aunt, so as not to frighten her mother's potential suitors away. "Whenever Mike, my stepfather, or any other guy would come around to see Mom," she told me, "she'd tell him I was just there to practice the piano."

Fanny, Lorraine's mother, was still a huge force in her life. Although she was in her thirties, Lorraine had just moved to an apartment of her own in the past year. This still caused arguments between them. "She comes over all the time," Lorraine told me, "to clean."

"To clean?"

"Yeah. And all the time she goes on about what a lousy housekeeper I am, why did I leave, and that it's dangerous for a young girl to be out on her own." Lorraine laughed as she spoke, but she was not entirely at ease with this situation.

I found this incredible on several levels, not the least of which was the concept of a small family. I am the ninth of thirteen children. I left home to join the United States Army at eighteen, my parents gladly giving me permission to enlist. Not only was there no shortage of brothers and sisters, but there was also a nonstop parade of nieces and nephews around our home.

I imagined Lorraine's family as an oasis of quiet and solitude, values I dearly cherish. But I found it even more incredible that a parent would clean an apartment for an adult child.

So, our family backgrounds were quite different. During the time Lorraine and I were getting to know each other better, her brother, Lenny, was going through what turned out to be a series of nervous breakdowns. I felt bad for him, innocently assuming that everyone in her family would be as kind and seemingly well balanced as Lorraine appeared to be. It also struck me that, with the sheer number of people and all the competition and tension in my family, it would be more logical to expect a nervous collapse from one of us. But there were none.

We'd spend our time at Lorraine's place in Midwood, near Brooklyn College, or at my place in Manhattan. I'd run out of money in England, and once in New York, I had to accept whatever living quarters I could find. After living in a miniscule hotel room for a month or so, I was able to find an apartment to share on 135th and West End Avenue. The catch was that my roommate was a man named Harry, an octogenarian painter who kept the place smelling of stale paint.

That wasn't the only flaw. Harry's part of the apartment was filthy. It took the army of cockroaches that also shared the apartment less than an hour to populate any boxed food that came into the apartment. Nothing could be moved in Harry's studio without creating a huge cloud of dust. When the dust cloud settled, the roaches would scamper with rodents and other insects of various sizes for places to hide. None of them had much trouble finding cover.

Nonetheless, Lorraine liked to come to my place. She didn't mind the mess, and found Harry to be charming and pleasant. The fact that Harry was an artist helped her overlook a lot. The work that Harry did was primitive to the point of childish, but it was also very dramatic, much of it dealing with Polish-Jewish partisans fighting German invaders. Harry liked Lorraine, too. The three of us had long conversations about art.

The neighborhood was still relatively safe at this time, and we both liked the apartment's proximity to Lincoln Center, but it got to where I was only spending one or two nights a week in Manhattan. Finally, we agreed that I should just as well move to Brooklyn and share the rent. I was there nearly all the time anyway.

FOUR

The move cemented us as a couple. It was the two of us, along with Lorraine's poodle, Juno.

One Saturday night, shortly after I moved into Lorraine's apartment, she invited two of her friends, Rebecca and Michael Silverman, over for supper. They showed up at our door with their two children: Tara, three, and Terence, five. From the outset, it was clear that Tara and Terence were put on this earth to test their parents, mostly by the use of the word, "No!"

When Lorraine opened the door, Michael said to his children, "Go in and say hello to Kenny and Lori."

"No!" Terence shouted as he turned to race down the hall.

Michael smiled and scooped up the fidgeting boy. "Just one minute, bub. We're going in here."

Terence shouted, "Hi, Kenny! Hi, Lori!"

Tara walked up to Lorraine and made grunting sounds as she held her arms out to be picked up.

"Lori is busy right now, Tara," Rebecca said, turning the girl away from Lorraine. "Go get your toys from Daddy and play with Terence."

"No!"

Tara grabbed her mother's hand and tried to bite it. Rebecca executed a perfectly timed dodge, which caused the undeterred Tara to grab Lorraine's leg and bite it instead.

"Ouch!" Lorraine cried, not doing a very good job of allowing politeness to hide real pain. "I didn't know kids this young had such strong teeth."

"Teeth! Teeth!" Terence cried as he ran toward Lorraine. He was moving his jaw up and down in anticipation of adding his marks to her leg.

"Just one second, bub," Michael said, catching Terence and pulling him off the floor.

"Hi, Lori! Hi, Kenny!" Terence yelled as he struggled to get out of his father's arms.

Rebecca gave a weary smile and unloaded a large burlap bag of children's toys. With a sigh, and to no one in particular, she asked, "How long will it be before I can send these kids off to college? Or, at least, how long will it be before I can go back to work? And whose idea was it to have two kids so close together?"

The children paid no attention to the toys. They were more fascinated with Lorraine's goldfish bowl. Their several moments of fascination gave Lorraine the opportunity to introduce me to the Silvermans, whom I hadn't met. We shook hands and got ready to sit down in the living room. The adult conversation ended abruptly, however, when Terence decided to stick his hand in the bowl and catch one of the fish.

"Look, Mommy, the fish is coming to me!" Terence was splashing water all over and pushing Tara away as she tried to get close enough to get her hands into the water, too.

Rebecca jumped up and dealt with this crisis as Tara came up and took my hand. "Baby," she said.

"I know you're a baby," I replied, "and a pretty baby, too."

"Baby!" Tara persisted, pulling my hand even harder.

"Do you mean, do we have a baby?" I asked her while looking at Rebecca and Michael for assistance.

"I think she wants to see your dolls," Michael said. "You do have a doll collection, don't you?"

"Oh, yeah, actually we do, sort of," I said. I got up and led Tara into the bedroom, where Lorraine had a few stuffed animals and a Raggedy Ann doll. Tara wasn't much interested in the animals, but the Raggedy Ann sure got her attention.

"Mine!" she screamed.

"No, honey," Lorraine told her. "It's mine. It belongs to me."

"Annie!" Tara screamed, getting even louder. She stomped her foot and waved her arms as though she were about to fly away. "Mine!" she shouted.

"I don't think she's saying this is hers," I said, handing the doll to Tara. "I think she's saying she has a Raggedy Ann, too."

"Good Lord, Ken," Rebecca said, "how did you know that?"

"I didn't," I said. "I was just trying to stop the noise."

The Silvermans—or, as their letters said, "Silvermen"—were a great couple. After things got a bit more settled, I learned that Rebecca was on leave from her job as a computer instructor and systems analyst at City College, and that Michael was a systems analyst at one of the largest brokerage firms on Wall Street. Both were also working toward advanced degrees. Michael had almost completed work on a master's, and Rebecca was writing her doctoral dissertation in mathematics.

Through intermittent bouts with the kids, we got to know each other. "Michael's given name is Moran," Rebecca said.

"Jeez," I said. "How'd you get such an Irish name?"

"Believe it or not, it's the last name of my parents' best friends. Yeah, it's a name I'm proud of," he said, "but it can be a real pain. When I use my real first name, most of my mail comes addressed to Moron Silverman."

We all laughed as Lorraine came in and announced dinner was ready.

During supper, Terence insisted on measuring the length of every piece of spaghetti by laying it on the table. Meanwhile, his sister scraped all the tomato sauce off her pasta and put it on her salad. Then she started throwing the salad at her brother.

"Young lady!" Rebecca tried to intervene.

Terence picked up the pieces thrown at him and threw them at Michael. These games were only stopped by a shout from Lorraine. The two children then engaged in a contest to see who could make the loudest noise drinking soda. Terence won easily.

After supper, it was time to walk Juno. The kids wanted to come along, and Michael and Rebecca were eager to let them go. So, off we went. At first, there was a tussle to decide who would hold the dog's leash. Juno settled that dispute by refusing to walk with either child. So Terence held my hand that held Juno's leash, while Tara held the other hand.

Terence was thrilled to be outside. First he counted all the red cars and then all the dogs. Then he started counting all the kids. The counting became a little complicated though. Anyone between his age and mine was counted as a "kid." Anyone Tara's age or younger was a "baby," and, thus, wasn't counted.

Tara talked constantly, with her brother sometimes acting as interpreter. She wanted to know who owned all the cars on the street. Did I go for rides in them? Which ones did I ride in? Did I see their car? Did I like it? What's that building? And on and on.

We came to a playground behind a Catholic school and both kids wanted to play on the swings and slides. After about thirty minutes of this, I told them we had to go home.

"Why?" Tara wanted to know.

"Your mom and dad won't know where you are," I said. "They will be worried."

"They're not worried," Terence said.

He was right. When we got back to the apartment, Lorraine was washing dishes. "Where've you been?" she asked from the sink.

"I let the kids play on the school playground," I said. "Are Rebecca and Michael worried?"

"You tell me," she said and nodded toward the bedroom.

Rebecca and Michael were on the bed, sound asleep. I closed the door.

Lorraine and I tried to entertain the kids by playing Go Fish, but Terence insisted on helping his sister and then took the opportunity to swipe from her whatever cards he wanted.

When they got to the Bronx, Michael called to thank us for "the most restful visit" they had had, anywhere, in five years. He went on to say that visits to both sets of grandparents were rigid and regimented. "It's supposed to be fair to everybody," he said, "but it isn't clear to me whom they're being fair to."

Rebecca got on the phone and told Lorraine that I was one of the few people who didn't seem angered or intimidated by the behavior of Terence and Tara. That was nice to hear, but Lorraine made it clear that we'd also like to see more of them, excluding the kids, at concerts, movies, or the opera, to "give the parents a nice break." Lorraine asked me if all children behaved the way "those kids" did. I assured her they did not, but she still said that having small children must take some "getting used to."

We did start to see more of the Silvermen on such occasions, but one time Terence called us to ask if he could come to see a play with us, too.

"No," I told him, "but maybe you guys can come on Sunday for a picnic in Prospect Park."

"Will you have any kids for me to play with?"

I laughed. I told Lorraine about it later.

"So," she said, "when are we going to have kids for Terence to play with?"

"Not until we're married," I said.

Lorraine gave a little cheer and clapped her hands. "Good!" she said. "I thought you'd never ask!"

Before we got married, however, I had to do the obligatory meeting with my future in-laws. Up to this time, I had heard a lot about them, but had never met anyone from her family; I had not even talked to one of them on the phone.

Fanny, Lorraine's mother, insisted that we come to her apartment one Sunday evening for dinner. Lorraine pleaded to go to a restaurant, but her stepdad, Mike, insisted on kosher meals and did not trust any of the restaurants in their area. Of course, their area was Brighton Beach in Brooklyn, which is at least ninety-percent Jewish, but Mike said they were all suspect, and he wanted to eat Fanny's cooking. She was the best cook in the world, Mike said.

Lorraine was a small person—just barely over five feet tall—but her mother and her stepdad were even shorter. They could be classified, in fact, as tiny. Lenny, in a moment of annoyance, called Mike "the world's tallest midget." Although I am only five-foot-six inches-tall, the first thing Fanny said after being introduced was, "I am glad to see you got a tall man, Lorraine."

Lenny and his wife, Henrietta, were also at the meal. Or, as Lorraine said, they were there "to share the pain." There was a tremendous amount of tension in the air, but it was not because of my presence. I immediately sensed tension between Henrietta and Fanny, and between Henrietta, Lenny, and Mike. Obviously, I had only just met the four of them, and I did not know the source of it, but the sniping got tiresome very quickly.

That tension was bad, but the food was worse. The matzo ball soup was very salty, and the matzo balls sank to the bottom of the bowl. Henrietta graciously pointed out to her mother-in-law that they should float and that there really was no need to cause a salt shortage every time she cooked a meal.

When the roast was served and proved to be extremely tough, Lenny joined in the carping and criticism. "I would have brought my power saw," he told his mother, "if I had known you were going to serve another of your granite roasts." He was also annoyed by the fact that the potatoes were burned. The complaining stopped when Lorraine said everyone should just shut up and "enjoy" the meal. Of course, immediately after that admonition, Fanny brought out yet another burned dish—this time it was corn and carrots that had gone through what Lorraine dubbed "the loving hands of the Queen of Burn."

After a short silence, Mike said to Lenny, "By the way, when did you get a power saw?" My laughter seemed to break the tension, and the rest of the excruciating meal was taken in relative calm.

Lorraine was silent the entire subway ride home from this meeting. When we were in bed, she said, "I hope that didn't totally turn you off."

"Well, I have heard about colorful families," I said, "but yours seems a little extreme. Maybe it is just my Midwest *goyisher* narrow-mindedness."

Lorraine started to cry. "No," she said. "It's not you. They are a real problem."

"Well," I said, "it is you I am marrying and not one of them. But I do hope you understand I won't be seeing much of that bunch."

Saturday, May 25, 1968 was a bright, clear spring day in New York City. It was our wedding day. We were married in fifteen seconds flat by a judge at City Hall in Manhattan. His beautiful benediction was, "I now pronounce you man and wife," followed by a brisk, "Next! Step in quickly, please!"

Our witnesses were my brother, Wil, and Henrietta. They were more nervous than we were. Wil kept jumping up as if looking for something, and Henrietta kept asking Lorraine how she was doing. "I am fine," Lorraine would say, "but I sure wish we would have gotten out of bed in time to eat breakfast. I'm hungry." Wil and Henrietta missed most of the actual ceremony because Wil held the door for Henrietta, who stood by it waiting to walk in the room with him.

Wil was the only one of my family who met Lorraine before we married. All my family was surprised by my marriage. Granny said she wasn't surprised that I'd considered marriage, since I had done that several times before; but she was surprised that I actually went through with one.

Wil was curious about Lorraine. Was she Jewish? She was. What was the difference in our ages? Lorraine was several years older than I was. "Well," my brother said, "none of that is important, unless you two use it to make trouble for yourselves."

I agreed with him. We were from different backgrounds. The age factor didn't have any significance. The religious difference was even less important. Lorraine's being Jewish was an administrative fact and had almost no bearing on her beliefs or behavior. In fact, as the years went by, it became clear to me that Lorraine was probably the least religious person I have ever met. To her, all religions were just so much hooey. She didn't keep a kosher house, which meant that her family, with the exception of her mother, never took a meal at our house. In simple truth, I never liked most of her family anyway, so this fact did not bother me at all.

And as for not "keeping kosher," Lorraine certainly did not do it for me. She loved pork products. I'm allergic to them.

I consider myself a Christian, but have come to the reluctant conclusion that most churches—at least the Protestant churches I've been to—are more organizational than Christian. I went to church and even got paid for singing in church choirs; but my Christianity is a personal matter, and I'm very little impressed by any church dogma.

I have to say now that Lorraine and I were naïve in our expectations of a married life with children, but no more, from what I have seen, than most couples. A family was our fondest hope. I have always been around and have always loved children. In the second month of our marriage, Lorraine became pregnant.

FIVE

Three things amaze me about Manhattan practitioners of medicine. One is the sheer number of them: every block seems to have several kinds of medical offices. Another is that they all seem to have enormous practices. The third thing that amazes me is the cost. All these medical men seem to have very positive concepts about their own value.

Expensive or not, Lorraine, who worked several years as a medical secretary, was impressed by an OB-GYN named T. Ian Balnick. Balnick was a small, intense man with an auditorium-sized office and practice near Fifth Avenue. He was of East European extraction; his medical training was taken primarily in France, and he spoke with a slight French accent, retained from his student days in Paris. Planned Parenthood had referred Lorraine to him before we were married and he had prescribed birth control methods for us. Going to Balnick meant Lorraine had to travel from the Midwood section of Brooklyn, where we had set up housekeeping, to midtown Manhattan. Balnick was also highly recommended by the doctors Lorraine worked for at a major research hospital in Brooklyn. He seemed to know his business, and because the pregnancy went so smoothly, I was pleased with him, too.

Lorraine started a new job, still as a medical secretary, immediately after we returned from our honeymoon. Because the pregnancy was so easy, she decided she wanted to work until the end of February. The baby was due at the end of March, and I made her quit work at the end of December.

I was certain we were having a boy. Lorraine insisted she was carrying a girl. I knew better, and made a deal with her to name our son George Marshall Zarecor, after my lifelong hero. She could name a girl, which I knew we were not having. Lorraine laughingly agreed, though she said the initials G and M could not be used. There is a Jewish custom that initials of newborn children are taken from the names of deceased family members.

We agreed that our child would be raised Jewish. I did not know then, and do not know now, exactly what that would entail, but I respected the Jewish religious law that states children born to a Jewish mother are Jewish. Obviously, in a "mixed" household where the Jewish member is the only consumer of pork products and the Christian member believes that true Christianity is almost never found in the so-called Christian churches, the religion of the children was not a wrenching decision. Our only thoughts were, in fact, about the easy pregnancy. We thought Balnick really knew his business, and we were going to be blessed with a healthy, active child.

Fortunately for Lorraine, her heavy months were in the cool of autumn and winter. As the pregnancy slipped into the concluding months, the child became increasingly active in the womb. The kicks it gave Lorraine could be felt and seen. Once, when we were both asleep in bed, Lorraine turned over onto her stomach. The baby did not like that position and gave a terrific kick that shook the entire bed and woke both of us up. Thereafter, Lorraine slept on her back.

One week before her due date, I took Lorraine to Balnick's office. He was as busy as ever but took us into his examination room at once. He was in excellent spirits and insisted that I listen to the fetal heartbeat. "It is a wonderful sound," I said, "something like hearing a frog croaking in a cave." Balnick looked confused, not understanding the allusion. "The fetus has not moved into position," he said. "I do not believe your child will be born on the due date of March 26."

"This isn't due to the fact I have a cold now, is it, Doctor?" Lorraine asked.

"The cold is not a problem," Balnick told her.

We went back home to Brooklyn.

March 26 arrived. Although we had been told not to expect the child, we were both apprehensive. I went to work as usual, but called Lorraine to check up on her several times during the day. She always felt fine, not as though she were about to deliver.

Ordinarily, I would have gone to jog around the indoor running track at the West Side YMCA in Manhattan before going home. But on this day, I thought I should go straight home from the office, and I did. Lorraine fixed supper for me, then lay down to rest. At about 7:00 PM she told me I should take her to the hospital. The baby was coming.

SIX

The cab ride from Brooklyn to French Hospital in Manhattan was filled with anxious moments. The cab driver grew so alarmed by the obvious pain Lorraine was experiencing that he wanted to take us to a Brooklyn hospital, not all the way to Manhattan. Lorraine's contractions, at one point, were only about six minutes apart. The cabby's obvious and loud distress at Lorraine's pain only added to our own discomfort.

Lorraine was clearly in intense pain, and we had several anxious moments including an attempt to get into the back door of the hospital, which was closed. We finally got into the hospital's main entrance.

After the usual check-in formalities, I was taken to a room close to the maternity ward. Lorraine was brought in shortly thereafter in a wheelchair. The nurse wheeling her told me to say, "Good night," and go home.

I was excited and confused, and I did not know any better, so I did as I was told. I got home about 9:30 PM.

By 2:00 AM, I had called the hospital several times. Each time, I got the same message from the maternity ward: "Dr. Balnick has been informed that Lorraine is in the hospital, but he has not yet come to the hospital. Lorraine is now in the labor room." The staff told me that they were getting calls from Fanny also, and that I should check with Dr. Balnick's office or wait until the hospital called me if and when something happened.

Balnick's answering service confirmed he had been informed by the hospital that Lorraine was in the labor room. I was told I could not talk to him personally at this time. The service would ask him to call me as soon as possible.

Sleep was erratic and poor. After calling three or four times and getting no information, I restrained myself from the constant calling. Finally, at 7:00 AM, I could wait no longer, and called Balnick's office again. The service said to call back at 9:00 AM. By now, trying to get some rest was senseless, and I couldn't hang around the house any longer. A better plan was to go back to the hospital and find out at the source what the story was. So, I dressed hastily and rushed back to Manhattan.

The back entrance to the hospital, which we had incorrectly tried to use the night before, was open, and I used it to get into the hospital. That entrance led directly to Lorraine's room in the maternity ward. The nurses on duty were not pleased to see me. After checking with the labor room and confirming that Lorraine was all right and that nothing had happened, they asked me to leave. I went back into the rear lobby for a cup of coffee to wait until 9:00 AM, when I could call Balnick's office again.

I called promptly at 9:00 AM. One of Balnick's employees answered the telephone. The only information she had was that Balnick had been informed about Lorraine being in the hospital. The hospital staff only knew that Balnick was not then in the hospital and had not been there at any time during the night, either. I demanded to know where Balnick was and what he was doing. The employee told me Balnick would call me back.

But Balnick did not call me back. After several more attempts, I finally reached him at noon. "What was the problem with the birth?" I asked. Lorraine had been in labor nearly fourteen hours.

"She was not, first of all, Mr. Zarecor, in labor," Balnick told me. "You and your wife should not have panicked the way you did. Why did you rush her to the hospital just because she was slightly uncomfortable?"

"She was in severe pain," I protested. "The contractions were only a few minutes apart. If she wasn't in labor, why did the maternity staff take her to the labor room almost immediately after she'd been admitted to the hospital?"

"The hospital tells me Mrs. Zarecor is not in labor." Balnick's tone was cold and his delivery clipped. "I am in contact with them constantly. I am an extremely busy man. You should not have taken her there."

"When are you going to see Lorraine?" I asked.

"I am a very busy man," he repeated. "When it is appropriate, I will go to the hospital."

I returned home and continued making hourly calls to the hospital and to Balnick's office. At four in the afternoon, Balnick's office told me he still had not been to the hospital to examine Lorraine, at least as far as they knew.

"What do you mean, 'as far as you know'?" I demanded.

The girl from Balnick's office hesitated. "He hasn't been to the office, either, Mr. Zarecor. He must be on—" the words were spoken hesitatingly, "—on other business."

I started to ask for an explanation, but the girl said quickly and rather loudly, "I'm certain he will call you when he has some news for you." She hung up the telephone before I could say another word. Another quick call to the hospital got me basically the same information. Balnick had been in touch by telephone, but he had not been at the hospital. When I asked why Balnick had not been to the hospital, they replied that he would go there "when he felt it was necessary."

Sensing that I had exhausted the patience of both the hospital and the secretaries at Balnick's office, I had Fanny make the calls. When she got no more information that I did, I had Henrietta call the hospital. The result was that none of us got any satisfactory answers.

Finally, at 7:00 PM, almost exactly twenty-four hours after Lorraine's first labor pains, Balnick called me. His tone was a higher pitch than usual and he spoke in a breathless voice. "Mr. Zarecor," he said, "I am at the hospital. I have to do an emergency Caesarean. I can tell from this X-ray I have in my hands that the baby cannot be born any other way. I am doing the operation immediately. You should come to the hospital at once."

He hung up. Other than saying "Hello," I had no other words in the conversation. After waiting for one very long day, the only information that I had was that an emergency operation was required to deliver our baby.

SEVEN

When I arrived at the hospital, I was taken directly to the room where Lorraine had been the night before. The nurse who had brought Lorraine into the room was there, making the bed in preparation for her return. "The operation is over," she told me. "Your wife is fine. You can see her very shortly."

It took a moment to hit me. If the operation was over, the child must have been born. Nervously, I asked if it was a boy or a girl.

"A girl," the nurse replied. She gave me a long, questioning look. "Have you been told about the child?" she asked.

"No, nothing. I only just got here. I only know what you just told me and what Dr. Balnick told me over the telephone."

As I was speaking, a second nurse came into the room. The first nurse touched my arm and began, "Mr. Zarecor, we—"

The second nurse, looking at the first, shook her head vigorously. She interrupted the first nurse. "Mr. Zarecor, Dr. Balnick should be here to talk to you momentarily. Please sit down and wait for him." Both nurses hurried out of the room, leaving the bed not completely made.

Of course, I couldn't just sit down. I followed them into the hall and then into a small office. "Are you sure it's a girl?" I asked. "And is everything all right?"

Both nurses looked uncomfortable. They repeated that I would have to wait for Dr. Balnick.

Balnick was not long in coming. He had an unlit cigarette in his mouth. That surprised me, since I had never seen him smoke before. When he saw me, he fumbled with a lighter and then the cigarette dropped out of his mouth onto the floor. He stomped on it. He gave me a quick glance, and then stomped on the cigarette again. Looking away, he began, "Lorraine is fine, Mr. Zarecor, but we ran into some problems with the infant. I have called in a specialist to look at her."

Still looking away, looking up and at nothing but walls and the ceiling in the room, avoiding my gaze, he continued. "I'm afraid we may lose her—the child, I mean. We'll do—have done—all that could possibly be done for the child, but we may lose her."

Before I could respond, another man, taller, older, and grayer than Balnick, came into the room. Balnick darted toward him. "Sam!" he shouted. "I'm very, very glad to see you! Let's go into the hall. I—oh, yes." Balnick seemed to remember that I was in the room. He waved in my direction. "This is the child's father, Mr. Zarecor. Mr. Zarecor, this is Dr. Sam Stein." Balnick grabbed Dr. Stein by the arm and led him out of the room before either of us could acknowledge the introduction.

Suddenly I was alone, unsure of what I'd heard. Unsure of what to think. Both doctors were back in the room in a matter of minutes. "Lorraine is being brought down now, Mr. Zarecor," Dr. Balnick said.

"How long will she have to stay in the hospital?" I asked.

"Ten or twelve days," Balnick replied. "Depending on how well the operation heals."

I looked at both doctors standing in the room. Balnick was disheveled and could not stand still. He was still avoiding looking directly at me. Stein was calm and seemed to be waiting for my questions.

"Are you going to take over the care of the baby, Doctor?" I asked him.

"Yes, if I have your permission to do so."

"Of course you do. We'll do whatever Dr. Balnick recommends. But when do you think we can take the baby home? Will she be coming home with Lorraine?"

Both men looked surprised. "Mr. Zarecor," Dr. Stein answered, speaking quietly and calmly, "you do not seem to understand. The infant is in grave condition. I thought Dr. Balnick had explained to you—"

Stein looked at Balnick as if waiting for Balnick to explain more fully what was going on.

Before either could speak, I asked, "Why is she sick? What is the problem?"

"We ran into medical problems," Dr. Balnick answered. "Medical problems that we could not possibly have foreseen. Dr. Stein is an outstanding man in his field. He will do—we will do—all that can be done for the baby." Balnick shook his head. He closed his eyes and took a deep breath. He opened his eyes and looked down at the floor. Seeing the cigarette butt that he had stomped before, he stomped it again. Balnick started to say something more, but instead turned and left the room. Stein stayed only long enough to ask how he could reach me if he had to.

Lorraine was brought in shortly after Dr. Stein left. She seemed to have aged ten years in the one day I had not seen her, but she was happy. "I'm so very tired," she told me. "Did they tell you? I heard them say 'the little girl is very pretty.'" She was asleep before I could answer.

I went to call our mothers. Granny was in Illinois at my brother Herschel's. Herschel's wife, Mona, had given birth to their second child, a girl they named Zhea, just two days before. Granny had, at that time, nearly forty grandchildren, and her first great-grandchild was about to be born. She listened very quietly as I told her what the doctors had told me.

"Kenneth," she asked, "are you all right?"

"I'm all right."

"Do you and Lorraine need anything? Any help?"

"I don't know, Granny. Right now I don't know anything."

"What you should do is get some rest. For whatever happens next. And let me know if there is anything Herschel or I or anyone can do. Be sure to let us know."

Fanny moaned as I repeated the doctor's words. She asked me to tell her again everything that had happened from the time I took Lorraine into the hospital. I repeated the sequence of events. She moaned again. After a pause, during which I could hear Mike in the background demanding to know what was wrong, she said, "Kenny, do you think something happened at the hospital? Maybe we should get another doctor to go to the hospital and check things out."

"What?" I asked. Fanny's questions intensified an already acute disorientation I was experiencing.

"Something's wrong, Kenny. Don't you see that? The hospital, or that doctor, did something wrong, something horribly wrong. Tell them we're going to send someone to see the hospital records. Or you take the records.

For the sake of the child, for Lorraine's sake, for your own sake, tell them you want the records and we are going to have this checked out."

"I can't do that, Fanny. You know I can't." I could not deal with any more of this.

"Oh, my God!" Fanny wailed. "My first grandchild! Something's happened to my first grandchild! Oh, my God!"

Mike's voice in the background got louder as he demanded once more to know what was wrong. And the thing was, I couldn't answer him.

Before I left the hospital, I was able to see our daughter. She was very tiny and very beautiful.

EIGHT

The telephone rang before 7:00 AM the next morning. I struggled out of bed to answer, wondering how anyone knew to call me just as I'd finally been able to get to sleep. I had a blinding headache and was barely able to stammer out a "Hello?" When I tried to rub my eyes to soothe them, I realized I had forgotten to remove my contact lenses before going to bed.

The caller was Dr. Stein. Once again, he was calm. "Your daughter had the trouble we expected, Mr. Zarecor," he told me, "but she pulled through the night. This hospital, however, isn't equipped to deal with her kind of problem. University Hospital, down on First Avenue, has the facilities and expertise we need. I'm also a senior consultant on staff with that hospital. With your permission, I want to transfer the baby down there. You'll need to come and accompany her. We need a parent to go in with the child."

"Dr. Stein," I asked, "what exactly is the problem with her?"

"At birth there was difficulty in resuscitating her. Now she will occasionally stop breathing spontaneously. University Hospital has excellent facilities and staff for dealing with such problems. Can you come?"

Within ninety minutes, I was back in the hospital. Formalities involved with the transfer were disposed of quickly. The staff was anxious to help get the baby to University Hospital as soon as possible.

I had trouble soothing my eyes, and they burned throughout the day. I am extremely nearsighted, and have worn contacts for many years to correct my poor vision. The events of the previous night and the day that followed were disorienting enough without having to deal with the fact that I could see very little or nothing. Much of the day, I felt like I was a nearly blind man struggling in a dark and menacing swamp.

I met Dr. Stein, who suggested that I tell Lorraine that the baby was being taken to another hospital. Lorraine was bright and cheerful when I went into her room, and she was pleased to see me. She asked if I had seen her the night before. I said I had, and she had talked to me. The conversation she remembered, but she was not sure to whom she had been speaking. Then she said, "I think they had trouble with the baby last night. One of the nurses said she kept them busy." I then explained about the trip to University Hospital. Because of her work in the medical field, Lorraine knew about University Hospital. She liked the fact that it is a teaching hospital, and said Stein was probably right that they could help the baby.

"Who, by the way, is Dr. Stein?" she asked.

"Some high-powered pediatrician Balnick called in as an expert to help with the baby."

"Did Dr. Balnick or Dr. Stein say what's wrong with the baby?"

"Only that she was having trouble breathing. Maybe I can find out more when we get to the new hospital."

Just before going into the room, one of the nursing staff gave me a form to be completed for the baby's name. I handed it to Lorraine.

"So, you're really gonna let me name her?" She laughed, remembering our bargain to let her name the baby if it was a girl.

"Yes," I said. "That was the deal."

"Have you seen the baby?"

"Yeah, I saw her last night."

"Is she as pretty as they say?"

"You haven't seen her?"

"No," Lorraine said. "A nurse promised to bring her in this morning, but they got too busy and couldn't, I guess."

I found this a little annoying, but rather than make a scene, I simply asked if, before going to University Hospital, I could take the baby into Lorraine's room.

The maternity staff readily agreed and allowed me to carry the isolette holding the baby into Lorraine's room on the way to the ambulance. We couldn't see her too well, but it was good enough for Lorraine to exclaim that the baby was, beyond question, the prettiest day-old kid in all of New York City.

A doctor accompanied us in the ambulance to University Hospital. The trip was uneventful, except for the doctor asking the ambulance driver twice to radio ahead to be certain that the hospital staff was ready to receive us.

Once at University Hospital, we were ushered immediately into the pediatric intensive care unit, where what seemed to be a small army of doctors, nurses, and attendants waited. I was introduced to all the people who were there. Several said consoling things, each of which only made me more anxious. The head of the group, Dr. Ryder, seemed to sense this, and instructed an attendant to take me to the admissions office. Dr. Ryder asked me to come back to his office in the pediatrics ward and talk to him after I had finished the admissions procedures.

I had been waiting to be processed in the admissions office for about thirty minutes when one of the nurses from pediatrics came to get me. When I told her I had not yet been processed, she took me directly to the supervisor of the office. The supervisor personally processed the admission, at the insistence of the pediatrics nurse.

Dr. Ryder was waiting for me back in the intensive care unit. He motioned me to come to him. I walked past the incubator the baby had been transferred to while getting to where Ryder stood. She was on her back, making jerking motions and a weak crying sound. But that wasn't what was alarming. She was a very deep blue from head to foot. I turned from walking toward Dr. Ryder and went to the incubator.

There, one member of the staff was commenting that the baby's color had improved. "Improved! Improved?" I gasped. "Her color has improved? What's going on here?"

Dr. Ryder took me by the arm. "You should come with me to my office, Mr. Zarecor."

I was too shocked to move, and Dr. Ryder had to nearly drag me away.

Dr. Ryder sat me down at his desk. "Would you like a tranquilizer or something to drink?"

"No, thank you," I said. "I just want to know what the problem is."

"Being a doctor is a wonderful thing," Dr. Ryder began, "but there are some awful things a doctor has to do. This is one of the worst—probably the worst. I can see, though, that you are young and strong. You can have more children." He took a deep breath. "Right now I have to tell you that this child probably will not survive another hour."

Never in my life, before or since, have I felt so hopeless or helpless. I lost all sense of where I was, why I was there, or how I could get away. Then came a feeling that I was being propelled out of this scene, being whisked somewhere distant and high. The quiet was profound. The light was intense and blinding, and all the objects around me were blurred and distant.

The sound of Dr. Ryder's voice intruded on this sense of disorientation and broke it up. He was talking about Dr. Stein being an excellent physician … if anyone could help …

"What's wrong, Doctor?" I interrupted him. "Is something wrong with me or with Lorraine?"

"No, Mr. Zarecor," he stated, "there's nothing wrong with you or your wife. In fact, you should have more children, as I have already told you. But …" Dr. Ryder paused. He never took his eyes from mine. It was as though he were trying to read my mind. Or trying to gauge the effect his words were having on me. I did not know what he read or saw, but he certainly pulled no punches with his next statement. Again, he looked me directly in the eye. "I'm afraid your doctor fucked this one up."

I did not understand. I did not want to understand. What was happening to our baby? I searched for some fact to latch onto, but instead I was again being pulled out of this place and time by a powerful, silent force that seemed to sweep me very high, very rapidly. Dr. Ryder's voice again brought me back to reality. "Does your wife know how endangered this child is?"

Another shock. I had to tell Lorraine our baby was going to die. Once more I began to sense a lack of contact with what was before my eyes, or of what I was doing there. All of this was too much. I was exhausted. I felt utterly defeated. Tears came, then sobs.

After I regained my composure, I said to Dr. Ryder, "No, I don't think she knows anything. I should call her and tell her. No—I should go and tell her."

Dr. Ryder was concerned for me, and was not willing to let me go back to Lorraine by myself. I insisted that I could go alone. I did not know how or why, but I had to tell her.

NINE

The maternity ward staff must have thought I looked like hell when I returned from University Hospital. The nurses offered me tranquilizers, coffee, soda, or even a bed if I wanted to rest for a while.

Lorraine asked only one question after I had told her Dr. Ryder's prognosis. "How long ago did they tell you this?"

"About thirty or forty-five minutes ago. Around eleven, I think."

Then she said very little, and sat staring straight ahead until Balnick appeared in the room a few moments later.

His was a bizarre performance. All the time he was in the room, he never stopped talking unless we interrupted him. It was as though he were afraid to stop. He would speak slowly, speed up, and then slow down again. Balnick could not have been with us more than ten or fifteen minutes, but he never looked directly at either of us. As he had done with me the night before, he only allowed an occasional glance in our directions.

"There was an unexpected end to the pregnancy ..." Balnick rambled. "Medical problems cropped up in the final minutes of the delivery ... these problems could not have been anticipated ... the chances are virtually a million to one ... the problem would never happen again ... Lorraine should rest for a month and you must have another baby immediately! Certainly within the next twelve months ..."

Finally, I interrupted him. "What exactly were the 'medical problems,' Doctor?" I asked.

"Medical problems," Balnick repeated. He sat in a chair in the corner of the room that was not near to Lorraine or me. Again he said, "Medical problems." He continued to talk for several more minutes but did not answer any questions we asked. As he spoke, his eyes darted around the room. He looked at the floor, and at the walls and ceiling, but he never looked directly at either of us. Finally, he rubbed the back of his neck with both hands. "I am not sure, not at all sure, that I can explain so you would understand." Suddenly, he jumped up and began pacing the room.

"I would understand, Dr. Balnick," Lorraine said quietly. "I have a lot of experience in the medical field."

"No," Balnick replied, still looking at the floor and walls, and not directly at her. He did not even seem to hear her. "I don't think I could tell you in such a way that you would understand."

He went back to the chair in the corner of the room and sat down again, but almost immediately jumped up. Still avoiding eye contact with either of us, he began to back out of the room. "Lorraine, I will check on you tonight …"

He was gone.

Fanny walked into the room shortly after Balnick left and the whole story was repeated. To my surprise, she was calm, and even said she was sorry that she had "bugged" me the night before when I called her from the hospital.

We talked for a while before Lorraine asked what time it was. We told her it was about 1:00 PM.

"Why?" Fanny asked her. "Are you hungry?"

"No, Ma. Kenny, go call. If they haven't called, it must be a good sign."

I called University Hospital.

"The baby's not in good shape," Dr. Ryder said. "But she is recovering from that spasm you saw." He paused before asking, "How are you doing, Mr. Zarecor?"

"I'm better, thank you."

"What about your wife?"

"She's very hopeful, but I don't know if she's really grasped the situation yet."

"That's understandable, I suppose," the doctor said. "I'll call you if there's any news."

"Well?" Lorraine asked when she heard me coming down the hall, even before I could get into the room.

"I think the signs are good," Lorraine declared after I recounted the conversation. "The baby's already lived longer than anyone said she could. So let's just assume that she'll be okay. We can fill out the form for her names."

Fanny shook her head "No," and started to say something, but I looked at her and indicated she should say nothing. We nodded at each other and both said, "Okay."

Lorraine wanted to name the baby Heather Clarice. The "C" of Clarice was the first letter of the name Clara, which happened to be the first name of both of our maternal grandmothers, and I suggested the name Heather Clara. And so Heather was named. Fanny said the "H" in Heather could be used in honor of my dad, whose given name was Herschel, and who died of lung cancer in 1965.

I stayed with Lorraine until nearly five. It was reasonably restful except for a horrible moment when University Hospital called just as we were both drifting off for some much-needed sleep. We both came out of our half-sleep with a start, but all the hospital wanted was for me to sign some forms that the admissions office had overlooked earlier.

After I left Lorraine, I went back to University Hospital. Heather was having another spasm, although this one was much less severe than the first one I'd witnessed. It was over shortly after my arrival.

Dr. Ryder introduced me to two more doctors, Dr. Lopez and Dr. Kahn, who were now in charge of Heather's care in the hospital. Dr. Stein still would supervise their efforts, but Drs. Lopez and Kahn would be managing her care, minute to minute.

Dr. Lopez reminded me of Balnick. He was somewhat darker but just as short and just as intense. I also noticed he had enormous hands. They were large enough to hide Heather when he held her. Of course, Heather weighed only six pounds five ounces, but hands that could hide her had to be large. Dr. Kahn was the taller of the two, always cheerful, and laughed a lot.

Dr. Lopez minced no words. "This is a child at severe risk," he said. "I'd put her chances at about one in two hundred or two hundred-fifty. She's connected to several machines, as you can see, and is being fed liquids intravenously from two bottles."

In the first of the two hours I was there, Heather's color returned to normal. The hospital staff seemed genuinely pleased that I was there and that Heather seemed to be improving. They explained to me in detail what was going on, and what were the good and bad signs on the monitors.

This nursing staff also seemed to sense that I was very near collapse all the time I was there. They again tried to soothe me with offers of doughnuts, coffee, food, tranquilizers, and comforting words. Among the comforting words were ones about University Hospital generally, and the team of Lopez and Kahn, working with Dr. Stein specifically. This group had "an excellent— better than excellent—record of saving babies."

Dr. Lopez also told me Heather had had one spasm every hour she had been there. Each spasm weakened her more, but each new spasm seemed to be less severe than the last one. He quickly added that he did not want to encourage me. The situation was still grave, Dr. Lopez said, "the baby is still in very critical condition."

As if to emphasize Dr. Lopez's words, an alarm on one of the monitors went off. Heather had stopped breathing again. As the alarm sounded, the area filled with people. Drs. Lopez and Kahn gave instructions to two or three of those who had rushed over to the incubator, and the rest of the staff stepped back to observe. Dr. Stein came in, and, after a quick appraisal of the situation, and after asking several questions and consulting the chart attached to the incubator, stated the right things were being done. He asked me to come into the hall to talk to him.

"I had a conversation with your mother-in-law," he told me. I couldn't judge from his statement, or from his tone, what his mood was, but I had a feeling he was not comfortable.

"Oh?" I said.

"She wanted to know if the baby would be normal if she survives."

"What? Where did she come up with that question?"

"I really wouldn't know. The question is, unfortunately, premature. There is no guarantee or even likelihood, for that matter, that this child will survive. What I wanted to say is, perhaps you should talk to your mother-in-law."

I did not feel up to talking to Fanny right then, and I definitely did not want to consider the implications of her question, but I called her anyway.

"Kenny, listen to me," she said. "I don't know what Balnick did, but he made a horrible mistake. He has horribly harmed the baby. I tried to find out from the hospital—"

"Which hospital?"

"Not University, Balnick's. I tried to find out what the chances are that the baby will be okay if she survives. Kenny, they are telling me nothing. That means they aren't saying anything because they don't know how terrible the damage is. Or they could be afraid to say. You could be left with a totally retarded child, a vegetable, or some other big problem. Kenny, tell the hospital not to take heroic measures to save her. If she cannot survive on her own, let her die. Have another baby. You're both young enough. Forget this baby."

I was so tired I could barely stand. Even holding the telephone in my hand took a supreme effort. Fanny was actually suggesting we let Heather die. Adding to this distress, I was now jolted into awareness that even if Heather were saved, she might have major problems.

There was no answer for Fanny. She was being preposterous. Who could conceive of letting a day-old infant die?

"Fanny," I said, "what you suggest cannot be done. It is unthinkable. We will first try to save the baby and then we'll see what happens and deal with it."

The next three days were long and tense. Lorraine was recovering well, except for a problem with her right leg, a problem that would persist for nearly three months. She was increasingly confident about Heather's chances. I was increasingly numb. Visiting Lorraine and Heather and keeping friends and family posted about mother and child was making me more and more tired. But the more exhausted I became, the less I was able to rest.

On the fourth day of Heather's stay in University Hospital, I met Drs. Kahn and Stein in the hall outside the pediatric intensive care unit. They were clearly pleased about something.

"Well, Mr. Zarecor," Dr. Kahn said, "you did it the hard way, but it looks as though you'll be taking a daughter home."

"You mean ..." I started to ask the obvious question.

"She's had no spasms for thirty-six hours," Dr. Stein said. "We feel her chances are now more in favor of surviving instead of the other way, for the first time."

"Oh, my God!" I exclaimed. "Wonderful! Let me go call Lorraine!"

"Do that," Dr. Kahn said. "But hurry back. We have a job for you to do."

Lorraine answered the telephone slowly. I later learned she had dreaded every telephone call for the past four days for fear of getting bad news. "I knew God would answer our prayers and that Heather would be well," she said.

The job Kahn had for me was to feed Heather a bottle. It was the first nourishment not given to her intravenously. She took the bottle eagerly and seemed very contented in her daddy's arms.

I had a daughter who would be well and who would be coming home.

TEN

Lorraine was clearly upset and angry when I entered her hospital room the day before she was scheduled to come home. She had been there nearly two weeks, and I'd visited her, as I had Heather, every day.

"What's wrong?" I asked her.

"You wouldn't believe what just went on in here," she said.

"Oh ... what?"

"An intern was checking me over. I told him I was going home tomorrow. He said, in that case, he'd just take out the stitches. So, as he was doing it, Balnick came in and raised hell. They were screaming and carrying on in here for twenty minutes. The Chief Resident came in and took them down the hall where they continued screaming for another half hour."

"Balnick must be feeling a lot of pressure, I guess."

"Not necessarily," Lorraine replied. "I heard another intern say that he thought everyone knew better. Nobody touches one of Balnick's patients. I think everyone around here is afraid of Balnick."

Heather remained in University Hospital nearly three weeks after Lorraine was discharged from her hospital. During those weeks, the hospital staff was more and more encouraged about her condition, but they also would occasionally drop alarming suppositions. The staff told me that the birth process had caused an intracranial hemorrhage. The respiratory distress noted might have caused the hemorrhage, but they did not know that for certain.

We were further told that tests indicated that Heather might be partially paralyzed on the right side. The tests were not conclusive, however.

Another test, inconclusive also, indicated that she might be totally or partially blind. And yet there were other complications. Heather did not have a grasping reflex, although, again, the staff did not know precisely what that might portend.

Dr. Lopez told me he was certain the apnea spells would continue. They might be brief—so brief that an untrained person might not notice them—but they would probably recur now and again. He did not think they would ever prove to be life threatening.

Still other possible complications were brought to my attention, but all the experts and tests could not confirm or deny the possibility of any kind of physical or mental problems.

Heather was discharged on a Sunday morning. On the Saturday before, Lorraine and I were invited to a conference with Drs. Stein, Kahn, and Lopez.

Dr. Lopez started by saying they were pleased and proud to be sending Heather home. They would feel much better about it if Lorraine had been able to come to the hospital to spend more time learning about the care of the child. This hadn't been possible because Lorraine, even five weeks after the Caesarean, was still experiencing pain and difficulty in moving long distances. I wasn't concerned, since I had been able to spend a few hours every day at the hospital.

"The important thing is your child is well enough to go home," Dr. Stein said. "To have saved this child's life is a major achievement, and we are proud of it. We also feel, however, that there are some things you should know about Heather's future."

"The future?" I suddenly had a vision of Fanny insisting that the child might be permanently damaged.

"The truth is," Dr. Kahn said, taking my arm, "that we don't know what the future holds. We have taken a large number of tests, and the results only indicate that we cannot predict, with any kind of certainty, what kind of development Heather might have."

Lorraine and I nodded.

"You have to understand that Heather can develop in any number of ways," Kahn continued. "She might be a totally normal child, mentally and physically. She could even be a genius or world-class athlete. Or she might develop up to the age of two or three, and then stop. We just do not know what is going to happen."

"What we're trying to tell you, Mr. and Mrs. Zarecor," Dr. Lopez continued for the team of doctors, "is that you should not be disappointed if Heather is slow in the first year, or, for that matter, is slow learning and developing throughout her life. Her development is something that cannot be predicted now."

"Neither Lorraine nor I have preconceived notions about how Heather should develop," I assured them. "We're just grateful to be able to take her home and to have a chance to 'parent' her, if I can use the word that way."

"Well, you'll certainly be able to do that," Dr. Stein said, as he stood up. "We want you to know that we are available for any questions, and we have an excellent pediatrician for you. His office is very close to where you live. Good luck to both of you, and to Heather."

There is really no way to thank people who did what this team of physicians did for Heather, but I tried anyway. Then I went and fed Heather her bottle and the first solid food given to her.

Lorraine's family—Fanny, Mike, Lenny, and Henrietta—came to celebrate Heather's homecoming that Sunday morning. The gathering did not impress Heather at all. She slept nearly all the time they were in the house. It was nice of her to take a long nap while they were in the house. It would have been nicer, however, if she would have been awake for them and slept for us during the night. We quickly learned that Heather did not know about napping. She would sleep for several hours and then be awake for a stretch of several hours.

Not only would she be awake, she would be awake to cry. And cry she did. From about 9:30 PM until the wee hours of the morning. I've been around many babies, but Heather had more stamina than any of them when it came to crying. She could and would literally cry for hours on end. On one especially bad day during her first week at home, she cried without let-up for nearly six hours.

We were becoming increasingly tense from worry and fatigue. It was impossible to get Heather to sleep nights. She would sleep during the day and cry all night long.

At the end of Heather's first week at home, I took her to Dr. Alan Halberman, the pediatrician recommended by Dr. Stein. They were about the same age, and, in fact, Halberman was near retirement. Although he had a large private practice, Dr. Halberman was also senior pediatrician, as was Dr.

Stein, at a major teaching hospital. He picked up "extra work," as he called it, by teaching courses at a medical school.

Halberman spent nearly an hour talking to me about our family histories while he examined Heather. He said he wanted to look at the University Hospital records again, and that we should come back in a week. He also suggested we try to keep Heather awake during the day, obviously, so she would—and we could—sleep at night. Keeping a month-old child awake when she wants to sleep is not easy, and it struck both of us as a mean thing to do, but we had to try it or go out of our minds.

On the appointed day, I returned to Halberman's office with Heather. She was sleeping, resting from a long night of keeping her parents awake.

Halberman examined Heather again, after awakening her. She had gained a pound since coming home, he said. That was a good sign. In spite of her hours of crying, she was gaining physically.

Suddenly, apropos of nothing, Halberman asked, "Are you planning to have more children?"

"Good Lord!" I exclaimed. "At this moment, Doctor, this one is about all both of us can handle. And if we don't get some sleep soon, we may not be able to handle her."

"Do you mean the baby is still crying all night long?"

"Yes, usually from around midnight to four or five in the morning."

"That will end, and fairly soon, I would think," Halberman said. "It's pretty clear from the hospital records why she is crying."

"Why?" I asked.

"The people at University Hospital gave her drugs to sustain her and keep her alive. Before she left the hospital the amounts had been reduced, but they were never stopped. Since she's been home, there's been no phenobarbital or any other drugs. She may be going through drug withdrawal."

"Isn't that hard on her—to take her off the drugs cold turkey like that?"

Halberman shook his head. "No. It wasn't cold turkey, really. Plus, she'd have to go through this sooner or later. It's likely she has only some level of discomfort now, and not real pain." He laughed. "In any case, the really uncomfortable ones are you and your wife, most likely."

I was too tired to laugh with the doctor.

Heather had started crying during the examination and was crying full volume now. Halberman, ignoring the screams, picked her up. "Are you and your wife planning to have more children?" he asked again.

"When Heather was born, Dr. Balnick said we should. We haven't talked or thought about it much since then. Why do you ask?"

"Who is Balnick?"

"He was Lorraine's OB-GYN man."

Halberman grimaced and shrugged his shoulders. "I can see why you might hesitate to follow his advice." He paused as he cradled Heather in his arms. She was still crying. He tried crooning to her, but his attempts to soothe her were not having an effect.

As he continued to cradle and sing to her, he looked at me for a long moment. It was as if he were trying to gauge my ability to absorb what he wanted to say. "You understand, Mr. Zarecor," Dr Halberman said, "I don't want to be the one who shoots holes in anyone's hopes and dreams." He stopped talking and resumed humming to Heather. She was unimpressed and continued crying.

After a few minutes, Halberman resumed talking to me. "I've known Sam Stein for many years. An excellent man, probably the best in the field. He says the prognosis for Heather is favorable. Well, I honestly do not see it. Because of the injury this child sustained at birth, I would say the chances of her ever developing in any way—physically or mentally—are virtually nil. If she should develop, it will be very slowly. For example, she might have the development of a two-year-old, but only when she's twelve or fourteen."

Halberman looked sadly at Heather as he rocked her. "A truly beautiful child," he said. "The saddest thing of all is, if I am right, your child has a very short life expectancy. In her condition, it's possible, maybe even probable, that she will not live to be a teenager. Now, since you and your wife decided to bring Heather home …"

"There was never any question but that we would bring her home, Doctor. Nobody had proposed another alternative before," I said, not attempting to hide my anger at the suggestion.

"I didn't mean, Mr. Zarecor, to get you angry or upset … well, excuse a stupid suggestion … it's dumb to think anyone would be anything but upset in this situation. But listen to me, if you still can. I'm trying to get you to see what is a realistic prognosis." He handed Heather to me. Inexplicably, she stopped crying.

Halberman laughed again. "I never cease to marvel at how children know who their parents are no matter how young the child is." He patted Heather. "What I am trying to tell you, and what I think would be a disservice for you and your wife not to know and understand is this: I think you are in for more heartbreak with Heather. God knows you've already had more than your share of that. Another child—even better, more children—would be a great help and support to you in dealing with what I am certain will come with Heather."

"We were told there is some possibility she might not develop, Doctor. But we aren't anxious to chance another trauma like the birth we just went through."

"There won't be another birth like this one. What happened to Heather had nothing to do with you or your wife. I'd be willing to stake my professional reputation on that. Any other children you have will be perfectly normal. Believe it."

Most of the things the doctors at University Hospital told me about Heather were not repeated to Lorraine until other doctors had also said them. I thought she was having enough problems just recovering from the operation and adjusting to taking care of the baby. I did tell her what Dr. Halberman said.

She did not address the question of more children. She asked, instead, if we should look for another pediatrician. We did not, but Lorraine would never take Heather to see Halberman. I always did.

Dr. Halberman retired in a year. By the time Heather had a new pediatrician, we were beginning to know he was right about Heather's development. We were also about to find out that, while many doctors had a firm idea that Heather's development would be minor or nonexistent, most of them had precious few concrete or usable suggestions to help her.

ELEVEN

Dr. Halberman recommended another neighborhood pediatrician, Dr. Roth. Roth was older than Halberman, but had no intention of retiring. Heather was fifteen months old when he first saw her.

Lorraine and I both took Heather for the initial visit to Roth. Heather's behavior was much as it was the day we brought her home, with the welcome exception that she would usually sleep through the night. The hours of crying still occurred, but less frequently. She gave no indication that she recognized us, or the sound of her own name. And there had been no indication that she might sit, stand, or walk.

Roth was a no-nonsense man, who did not let the possibility that he might come off as offensive stop him from giving us a dose of candor. After giving Heather a number of shots, he gave us his version of reality.

"On the basis of the medical records I've seen, I have no idea how anyone would have suggested bringing this child home, let alone that you might expect a normal or nearly normal child. It just goes to show you that the so-called brains in the field can be as wrong as the rest of us."

"Dr. Roth," Lorraine spoke very softly, speaking as if she didn't want to disturb him, "isn't there something we can do to help stimulate Heather's development?"

"Listen, I am not trying to be, and don't want to be, harsh or cruel, but this child …"

"Heather," Lorraine interjected, still speaking quietly.

"Yes, Heather," Dr. Roth agreed. "This girl suffered damage at birth that means the chances are at least a thousand or a million to one that she'll ever develop."

"Doctor, isn't there some way or somebody to help?" I asked.

"We can have her checked by a number of experts. I suppose we should do that, for that matter. Although, you should understand, all these tests will probably—almost certainly from what I see—will lead you to nothing but more pain, anger, and disappointment. What I'm hammering away at is for you to understand one thing. The baby ..." He glanced quickly at Lorraine. "Heather, that is, is almost certainly profoundly retarded physically and mentally. Just feel her head: it's probably harder than yours or mine. The head has to stay soft so the brain can grow. That means, well, it probably means, she will not even grow to normal size. The chances of her developing motor skills, or of being toilet trained, even—in other words, the possibility of her ever doing even the most mundane of tasks for herself—are virtually nil."

Lorraine tried to interrupt him, but Roth continued speaking. "You must know all these facts now. And you must understand them now. As she grows older, she will become a burden, then a bigger burden, and then an intolerable burden. You will be able to keep her at home only with the greatest of personal sacrifices. Even if you had more money than Rockefeller—and you don't, do you? —you will make great sacrifices if you try to keep the girl, uh, Heather, at home. And—and I want you to understand an institution would probably take better care of her than you could hope to, simply because they have the expertise to do it."

"Doctor," Lorraine continued to speak very softly, but her voice had a steely edge in it, "we will not consider anything of the kind, now or in the future." She looked Roth straight in the eye, and started to say something else. Instead of speaking, however, she simply shook her head and then shrugged her shoulders before continuing. "Where do we go in order to try to help Heather?"

"I'll have some appointments made for you with specialists in the field of pediatrics. My wife will call you with the times, dates, and addresses." Dr. Roth smiled. Neither Lorraine nor I returned his smile. "I hope you will forgive my speeches and lectures. But I do want to make sure there is a clear understanding here."

"There is," I answered. "As my dad would have said, we're hoping for the best, but preparing ourselves for the worst."

I expected Lorraine to start looking for a new pediatrician, but she did not. Soon we were taking Heather to what seemed like a different doctor every week for some kind of evaluation. The first doctors were ophthalmologists. We saw three. All three said Heather had normal optic nerves, but they were not developing, and because they were not being used, they would atrophy. She would be, or already was, blind. She did have a startle reflex—she would react when a light was shined in her eyes or when a light was turned on in a dark room, but her eyes never followed the light. After a few years, even the startled reaction ceased.

Heather's left eye was crossed, and two of the ophthalmologists wanted to do a simple operation that would correct it. We declined because we felt she was going through enough without having an operation that filled a cosmetic purpose only. All three doctors we consulted said there was a less-than-zero chance this surgery would do anything to stimulate her vision: in other words, there would be no change in her sight. Another concern we had was how she would physically tolerate any operation.

One of the more memorable visits was to an X-ray diagnostician. I had to hold Heather down, while the poor technician endured her screams. Heather would not move a lot, but she could wiggle enough to require the technician to retake shot after shot. After all this agony, the expert had nothing new to offer. He did prescribe a body brace to help correct Heather's scoliosis. Everything else he said we had heard before, including his slant on the very serious problem we had on our hands and would face in the coming years.

We went to a number of neurologists, including Dr. Fisk, a doctor who worked and taught at University Hospital, the hospital that had saved Heather's life. Fisk was a man in his early thirties, but he was already a professor on the university's faculty. During our first visit to his office, he examined Heather for nearly an hour. He tried to obtain physical responses by waving things in front of her, by squeezing her, and by tapping various parts of her body.

When he was through, he asked us if we knew the degree of Heather's retardation. He indicated I should take her from him.

"She is over a year-and-a-half, Doctor; and she does not sit up, walk, or seem to recognize any specific sounds. If a sound is loud, she might cry or act startled, but she never looks in the direction of the noise. She does not respond visually, except to jump whenever a light is turned on in a dark room. We know the retardation is bad, but we're trying to find some way or some place to stimulate her, and maybe reverse some of it."

"I can suggest some programs for her, but I still wonder if you know how serious the problem is."

"I don't see what you mean, Doctor," Lorraine said. Her eyes narrowed and she closed her lips tightly.

"Look," Dr. Fisk gestured as if to indicate he were being forced to say something that should be obvious, "your daughter is around eighteen months old. Her responses are negligible to virtually any stimulus. We have to face the facts. And the facts, frankly, are these: from what I can see, and from what the other doctors you have been consulting have told you, Heather will never walk, never sit, never feed herself, never dress herself. I can go on and on about how dependent Heather will always be, but you surely know by now she will be totally dependent for every life-sustaining activity for as long as she lives."

"She's only a baby, Doctor." Lorraine's head was bowed, her eyes nearly closed.

"She's only a baby now. But she is getting older and she is getting larger. As long as she survives, she …"

Lorraine sounded and looked as if she were choking. She fell forward in her chair. I grabbed her and pulled her upright. She took Heather from me and held the child closely and tightly.

"Lorraine," I asked her, "do you want to leave?"

"Maybe we should. The baby shouldn't have to hear any more of this. I'll be downstairs in the lobby." Lorraine quickly gathered Heather's things and, after mumbling a good-bye to Dr. Fisk, left.

Dr. Fisk shuffled uneasily in his chair. "I don't know that there is another way of saying what has to be said, but I really didn't mean to upset her."

I shook my head. "If we're going to be honest about this situation, I guess there's no choice, Doctor. But now you should finish what you were saying."

"What was I saying?" Dr. Fisk moved from side to side in his chair. He picked up and discarded papers on his desk.

"I think you were talking about how Heather would be totally dependent as long as she lived."

Fisk nodded his head. "I would say, given her problems and the state of the medical art today in dealing with children who have her kind of problems, it is very likely that Heather will survive until her early teens—thirteen or fourteen. Her life span could be from, say, ten to fifteen. By the age of thirteen or fourteen, the body will be so weak from her associated illnesses and problems that any simple, common cold—or any other common illness—flu, for example—could bring her end."

I could feel myself getting angry, but struggled to contain it. "How does one arrive at such a prediction, Doctor? I mean is it an absolute finding experienced by all the men in your field? Is it based on some medical formula? How do you decide such things?" I realized I was speaking loudly, angrily. Then the thought occurred to me that I should not be angry with Dr. Fisk. He had done nothing but try to explain the situation as he saw it, and he was speaking from the perspective of an experienced, talented professional. "I'm sorry, Doctor. I don't mean to sound hostile to you."

Dr. Fisk was neither surprised nor upset by my anger. "If you did not feel anger, something would be wrong. I just hope the anger goes into productive channels. We can get Heather into programs to see if she could be stimulated. That would be the most constructive thing we can do now."

TWELVE

Consultations with specialists of all kinds continued. None of the experts offered any kind of hope or encouragement. One of the more dopey ones, a physical therapist, informed us that the best thing we could do for Heather was to keep a positive attitude, so that the "vibes" around her would always be "soothing and warming." At that point, I was beginning to feel that we had met with all the sane and rational experts and, having received neither help nor good news, had passed into the area of the kooks and weirdos.

We did enroll Heather in various physical therapy and stimulation programs. Most of these programs were in Manhattan, so we moved there to be close by them. Our apartment was too expensive and too small, but Lorraine loved the idea of living on West End Avenue. It was the fulfillment of a dream for her.

Heather did not show any sign of mental development, but there were small physical improvements. She became more active and was finally able to turn herself over. Sometimes she would manage to roll around a little, especially if she was being played with. For the first time, she would respond to being tickled. When left alone, she would ordinarily lay still and make no sound, as if in her own very special darkness. She could do nothing to feed herself, but her appetite was excellent. She ate very well, and she ate a lot. She could not hold her own bottle.

Specialists and the therapy groups that worked with Heather began classifying her as a victim of cerebral palsy, a designation that made Lorraine angry. Cerebral palsy, a general term indicating developmental problems, attempts no designation as to the cause of the problem. It is only meant to designate certain involuntary motions and difficulty in controlling voluntary muscles.

Lorraine was kept busy taking Heather to her various therapies while attending classes at Hunter College. My income kept us out of some programs, but because Lorraine was a student, a city agency provided babysitters while Lorraine attended class.

I took Heather to the therapy when I could get away from work. Lorraine dreaded most of the sessions. She bore the brunt of getting Heather there and staying around to observe what went on. She began to beg off and miss more and more sessions. This reluctance to take Heather for physical therapy became the point of some contention between us.

"Heather always cries," Lorraine told me, "from the time we leave the house until the time we get back home. Why do we have to torture the baby? All of this is not doing so much good that the baby has to be tortured."

Once, after I had taken Heather to a physical therapy session at a large Manhattan hospital that had a prestigious cerebral palsy program, I exercised Heather in her bedroom, as the hospital staff had suggested we do.

Heather was crying bitterly, as she had done at the therapy session. Lorraine hovered anxiously as I stretched Heather. She then began pacing, doing a mincing little step.

"Can't you see she doesn't like that?" Lorraine said, grabbing my arm to pull me away from Heather. "You're hurting her."

"The hospital staff said we should do this and do it often," I told her. "What I see is that you can't take her crying. You don't want to try to stimulate her because you can't stand listening to her cry. Just who the hell benefits if she doesn't cry but never does anything?"

Lorraine let go of my arm. "You don't understand. You don't have to listen to her cry hour after hour. You don't care if she cries anyway. All that pushing and pulling is doing nobody any good."

"If you don't like it, why don't you leave the room and let me finish what I've started?" I asked.

"No! I won't! This is my child. I am not going to let you or anyone else punish her ..." Lorraine tried to push me away as she grabbed for Heather.

I lifted my right hand and struck Lorraine across the face. That gives her the sole and dubious distinction of being the one and only person I have struck in anger as an adult.

To strike any person for any reason is hardly an achievement. To strike a person as gentle and as kind as Lorraine is probably horrendous. Still, I cannot say I am sorry, even all of these years later.

I am not sorry because that one slap had a bigger effect than all of my begging, pleading, and arguing with her. After that slap, Heather never missed a therapy session unless she was ill. Lorraine could never bring herself to exercise Heather, in spite of repeated suggestions of the program staffs that it would help Heather. Lorraine also let me try to duplicate the therapies in our home without a word of protest. She usually left the room when I did the exercises, and did so long after Heather stopped crying during them. She never uttered another word of protest on the subject, either.

The success of the therapies was not great, but it was real. Heather's right side was partially paralyzed, but her left hand was stimulated and strengthened enough to allow her to take her own bottle by the time she turned three. She began to play with toys in her crib and would take articles from our hands and play with them momentarily and then give them a toss.

Our primary contact with Heather was through sound. Once the physical stimulation started to show results, Heather also began to respond to different sounds. Touching Heather would sometimes, but not always, bring a vocal response from her. If a babysitter was holding her and Lorraine or I came into the room and spoke, she would whine or cry until we took her. When another person came into the room and spoke, even if the words were spoken to Heather, she would not respond.

We were pleased to see these small changes and hoped we were seeing the start of dramatic improvements.

THIRTEEN

Shortly before Heather was two, just before we moved to Manhattan, Fanny called me at the office. "I think you and I should talk about little Heatherel," she said, using the affectionate Yiddish form of her name.

"I have to be in a meeting in one minute, Fanny. Can I call you back?"

"No, don't call me back. It would be better if you came to see your old mother-in-law. Why don't you do that Saturday, when you're out on your bike ride?" Fanny was not asking a question, she was clearly issuing a summons to appear before her.

"I could do that, I guess. But why don't you discuss whatever it is with Lorraine, and then she can discuss it with me."

"I've been talking to Lorraine, but she doesn't want to hear. We should do something about what happened to the baby."

I knew what it was she wanted to discuss. Fanny had been telling Lorraine that we should see an attorney about the events at the hospital when Heather was born. Either Balnick or the hospital, or both, had bungled the birth and we had been handed a severely damaged child. That wrong had to be redressed in a lawsuit.

Lorraine's answer was always that nobody knew if or how Heather would develop. Many children do not walk until after their first birthday. The latest medical opinions we were getting, and the medical opinions we had gotten, were all dismal. Still, Lorraine said, they could be just as wrong as that first prognosis I was given that she would not survive more than a few hours. We should not lose hope in Heather's future.

I did agree that we should not lose hope, but I also pointed out it was becoming impossible not to credit what all the doctors were now saying. By this time, we had seen nearly twenty-five different experts in various fields. Not a single doctor had predicted any kind of development for Heather. Nearly every one of them, some as gently as possible, but most with cold, thrusting harshness that stuck me as intolerance, had told us there was virtually no hope for "this child." Period. End of story. How long were we going to continue to deny or evade all of this expert opinion, and, in fact, what we were seeing and experiencing ourselves?

No, Lorraine would say. We are evading nothing. We should not write Heather off. She was as much a person as anyone else and should be given as much a chance as anyone else. Heather would fool all the doubters and nay-sayers again. And Lorraine felt that to institute a lawsuit would be an admission that the doubters were right. Precisely how discussing the feasibility of a malpractice suit had any bearing on Heather's development escaped me, but Lorraine got upset and angry if the subject was brought up.

Dave Waller, an attorney who did legal work for the real estate firm I was now working for, told me he had done business with one of the best malpractice firms in the city. If I wanted, he would introduce me. When I asked Lorraine if she thought we should take Dave up on his offer, she said she absolutely would not go, and I shouldn't either. Even considering a lawsuit was premature.

Knowing what Fanny wanted and would say, and honestly not caring to hear it, did not increase my pleasure as I rang her doorbell.

After letting me in, Fanny gave me grape juice. "Drink it slowly, bubbala," she told me. "The drink is cold."

Fanny asked me why Lorraine never came with me on my bike rides. I told her, as I am sure she knew, that Lorraine couldn't ride a bike. Then I recounted the time I had tried to teach her to ride. To begin with, I would hold onto the bike and walk beside her, and then let go of the bike if I thought she was doing well. When she realized I was not holding on, she would fall off the bike almost immediately. After being knocked down twice in one day by these falls, I told Lorraine she had had enough for that day, and ended the session. She never asked to try again, and I never volunteered to give her another lesson.

Fanny thanked me for coming. If I had come earlier, she said, she could have gone to the beach, but it was nice of me to come. A son-in-law should not be a stranger in the home of his wife's mother.

Getting to the point, Fanny said, "I want to talk to you about two things, Kenny. The first is poor little Heatherel. How do you think she is doing?"

"Unfortunately, she's doing very little. The unanimous verdict among the professional people we are seeing is that she never will do very much. I thought Lorraine was telling you all of this."

"She did tell me things the first few times she took Heatherel to a doctor, but not anymore. Now all she'll say is that every doctor we see is only interested in getting his consultation fee. All they want is to get rich and none have any interest in helping Heather."

I shrugged my shoulders. "Lorraine is a very optimistic person," I said. "It is as though she thinks keeping a good thought will help Heather do all those things you expect a child to do."

"What do you think, Kenny?"

"Well, it's very hard for me to expect anything but the worst after being told by twenty or thirty different doctors there is no hope for Heather to develop normally or even develop at all, for that matter."

Fanny took my empty glass and walked back to the refrigerator to refill it. I realized again how small she was—she had to stretch to reach the top shelf of her normal-sized refrigerator. She returned with the drink and sat across from me at the kitchen table. I smiled to myself as she hoisted herself onto a chair. Her feet could not touch the floor. Fanny leaned forward and smiled back at me. "Does your old mother-in-law amuse you?"

"No, no," I said, stammering out the dumbest possible answer. "I just find it very pleasant here."

"Well, you could certainly come more often," she said. "But then I know you're busy." She smiled again. "Anyway, we were talking about Heatherel. Do you remember what happened the day she was born?"

"Of course I do."

"Have you ever thought that butcher of a doctor—no, 'doctor' is too good to call that fiend—and that has-been hospital fouled up and may have hurt the baby?" Fanny referred to the hospital as 'has-been' because it was about to declare bankruptcy and close.

"I have," I said. "Many people I've talked to about Heather tell me we should have an attorney look into the birth. I've thought a lot about it, and even have a referral to a good malpractice firm, but Lorraine seems to think going to an attorney is tantamount to condemning Heather to her present state."

Fanny shrugged her shoulders and shook her head sadly. "She can't really face up to the facts, I'm afraid. That's why she keeps going to more and more new doctors. Like I've tried to tell her—how many eye doctors or neurologists have to tell you there are serious problems with your child before you begin to believe them? I know how she feels. It's so painful. My one and only grandchild. My daughter's baby. I know the pain, Kenny. Other people have dozens of grandchildren and not a single one of them has any kind of problem. I have one, only one, and she is ruined, ruined by some—"

"We really don't know that she is ruined, Fanny."

"Oh, come on, Kenny! Surely even you don't think something or somebody will magically touch Heatherel and she is going to all of sudden start walking and talking? We have to face the facts, and the facts are—"

"I don't know, Fanny. As I said, there is not much cause for optimism, but that doesn't mean we should give up hoping and trying."

Fanny put one of her hands to her head and moaned. I could not help but think that, after listening to several doctors who seemed to take real pleasure in delivering bad news, I was now being subjected to a very poor Theda Bara impersonation. "If you have to give up hoping in order to do what should be done, then you should give up hope. Hope that flies in the face of what's really happening and what should be done will, in the end, only hurt everyone involved."

"What is it that you think we should do, Fanny?" I knew it was a dumb and obvious question, but I thought that by guiding the conversation, I might be able to end it and escape.

"Go to a lawyer, Kenny." Fanny was pounding the table. "Let them find out what happened when Heather was born. If they can prove what I think they will be able to prove, let them proceed against Balnick and his crappy hospital."

I shook my head. "No. No. Not now. What you say, Fanny, isn't wrong, but I'm not sure I can or should go ahead as long as Lorraine is so set against it."

Fanny pointed a finger at me. "You're the man in the house, Kenny," she said, "and you'll have to take the responsibility and lead and just go ahead. She won't listen to me. She won't listen to you. She isn't listening to anybody.

And what neither of you seems to understand is that you have only a certain amount of time after the birth to take action. You are wasting time and are in danger of losing all your rights to damages."

Again I shook my head. "No. She doesn't seem to be listening to anything she doesn't want to hear. That's certain. Any lawsuit without her help and acquiescence would be senseless and would be bound to fail. Maybe she is right and Heather will surprise us all. That, even to me, is a completely unrealistic hope, but who is to say one way or the other? At this moment, all we can do is wait and see."

"You are going to wait so long your time to do anything will have passed," Fanny said very loudly. She clearly was not satisfied with my answer. "You have to realize you only have so much time to file a lawsuit about Heather. And damage was done to you and to Lorraine, too. You need—you deserve—compensation for yourselves and for Heather! You should not let those butchers just walk away from this crime!"

For a few minutes, Fanny did not speak. I stood up, ready to leave.

"Aha!" Fanny said, still speaking very loudly. "You and Lorraine are both experts at hit-and-run visits. There is something else we need to talk about, Kenny. You should learn to relax when you're a guest in someone's house."

I almost laughed out loud. Fanny was shouting at me that I should learn to relax. She obviously had a strange conception of relaxation or how to get someone to relax.

"You should not begrudge your old mother-in-law the chance to talk to you," Fanny said, speaking at a more conversational volume.

"I don't, Fanny. What else did you want to talk about?"

"Children, Kenny. Another child. Have you and Lorraine considered having another child?"

"We've talked about it," I said. We had, but only indirectly. Lorraine asked her doctor about bearing more children. The doctor told her we should not consider that until she lost some weight. Lorraine now weighed more than she did when she was carrying Heather, and she said that she just was not up to dieting now.

"Well?" Fanny said.

"You know," I told her, "several of the doctors who have examined Heather said we should have more children. But as long as Lorraine is as heavy as she is, another pregnancy is out of the question. It could be dangerous both to her and her baby."

"So can't you encourage her to lose weight?"

"I do and I have tried to talk to her about it, but trying to push or harass her would only lead to frustration for both of us. We also should not expect her, I think, to do anything that might force a decision about Heather."

"What? What decision? What do you mean?"

I looked at Fanny and wondered if she really did not understand the possible ramifications of one or more additional children to the care of Heather, or if she just wanted to know what I had on my mind.

"Suppose," I said, "we had another child or two. Suppose also that Heather remains totally dependent, as it looks more and more every day like she will. More children could conceivably put us into a position of institutionalizing Heather. In other words, we might have to decide that the welfare of one child is more important than the welfare of another. That is a choice Lorraine would never be able to make, and I am not at all certain I could make it, either."

Fanny returned to her Theda Bara mode. She sighed, rubbed her eyes and forehead, and uttered a long, low moan. "You surely realize," she said, "that sooner or later you will have to put Heatherel away—" When she saw the look on my face, she leaned back into her chair, as if afraid I were about to strike her. She continued. "I mean, put her into some kind of 'home' sooner or later, with or without other children. Why do you keep putting it off? Doing what has to be done isn't going to be easier next year or in five years. The longer you wait to do the inevitable, the harder it will be."

"Obviously, if it is to happen, whenever it happens, placing Heather in an institution will not be an easy thing to do." I felt a strong urge to leave, to end this discussion.

Fanny seemed to sense my agitation. The anger had gone out of my face. She leaned forward and patted me on my hand to comfort me. "Lorraine will need your strength to do what is best for herself and for the baby. It will be very hard, but I know Lorraine, and I know you will probably have to do something like that on your own."

"Something like that on my own?" I did not mean to mimic Fanny, but that is probably what she thought I was doing when I repeated her words. "I probably could force the issue, but it is much too early to even consider that."

"You're going to wait until both your lives are totally ruined. Ruined!" Fanny shouted. "And you will be doing the baby no good, either. You need to act now, put Heather in a state institution and start the lawsuit. You must do both!"

Again Fanny was telling me what I should be doing. She had a very clear idea of what was right and wrong in this matter. Fanny felt she was right, so we should do as she said. Not only did I feel her words were condescending and demeaning, but I felt she had no business dictating a course of action involving our child, even if she was the grandmother of Heather, and Lorraine's mother.

I moved toward the door. "First of all, Fanny, legally or morally I could not force Lorraine to give Heather up. Second, even if I could, I would not. Third, only the parents of a child should be the ones to decide the future of their child."

Fanny looked momentarily helpless. I grabbed the opportunity to leave.

FOURTEEN

When I told Lorraine about my conversation with Fanny, she slammed the plate she was holding onto the kitchen table. "I wish she could try to help instead of meddling." After a pause, she started to say something else, but stopped. After another short pause, she told me she might be pregnant again. "My period is over six weeks late."

"Have you been to the doctor?" I asked.

"No, but if something doesn't happen in the next two or three weeks, I will go."

"Have you had any ill effects, like morning sickness?" Lorraine was giving me no clue about her own feelings about another pregnancy.

"A little discomfort. I seem to get carsick easily, but basically that's all." Lorraine looked at me for a long minute. "Do you want another baby?"

"It would make me very happy," I said, causing Lorraine to brighten considerably. She was afraid I'd be angry. "We should find an OB-GYN," she said. She was not working, but the doctors at her last job could recommend someone good, she said.

Going to her old job for a recommendation was not a good idea, I thought. These same people had highly recommended Balnick. That was not, however, the major issue that concerned me: Lorraine was now heavier than she had been when she was carrying Heather. She didn't believe she was too heavy. Lots of heavy women have perfectly healthy babies.

A week later Lorraine told me she had talked to Fanny about Heather. "Ma said Heather would have to be institutionalized if there were another baby, and we should not wait any longer and start that process right now."

"Your mother told me it would have to be done sooner or later even if we didn't have another child," I said.

"Do you agree with her?"

I shook my head. "Not necessarily, but I don't really know. It does occur to me that the way things are going, we may be forced to consider what will be best for Heather and what will be best for us. You know, there are three parts in this equation—there is Heather, there is you, and there is me. Each one of us has to be considered in deciding what will be best for Heather. It certainly is possible that an institution could be an answer, but, as I say, I don't know yet. Neither do you, and your mother certainly doesn't know."

"No, no. An institution is not an alternative. We can take care of Heather." Lorraine looked more fearful than angry.

"Honey, there's something that you have to understand. How can you be expected to handle a normal-size teenage girl? She may be as tall as you are and may be completely dependent. Actually, she could grow to be taller than both of us are. Who knows? It is not realistic to expect you to be able to handle that kind of a burden."

"Heather is not a burden." Lorraine's blue eyes darkened, and her voice rose as the fear I noticed earlier was turning to anger. "She's so small, so helpless. We can't give her up. What person in the world could do something like that?"

"I'm not saying she is a burden. What I am saying is neither you nor I may be able to properly care for a totally dependent child who grows to be adult or near-adult size."

"Heather is not a burden," Lorraine repeated, angrily emphasizing each word. It was clear that Lorraine could not consider this subject now. There seemed to be no sense in continuing a discussion in which things would be said that could further anger and possibly alienate her. I said no more. Lorraine took Heather into her bedroom, slammed the door, and did not come out of the room until the next morning.

After this conversation, I could tell that Heather's future was never far from Lorraine's mind. She would frequently repeat stories about families we both knew who kept handicapped children at home. Since I also knew the families Lorraine talked about, I also knew there were some differences in circumstances. First, none of the "children" were, in fact, children. They were nearly all over twenty. Most were ambulatory, and all had some speech abilities. They all had enough ability for training to do simple household tasks or menial jobs. One was a part-time janitor; another worked in a school cafeteria. Even this limited hope was wildly beyond what seemed to be realistic for Heather's future.

Lorraine was still unwilling to even concede that Heather might be profoundly retarded, physically and mentally. It was politically incorrect then (and is probably more so now) to call any person "retarded," and Lorraine never used the term. I did use it and do use it, simply because it is the medically and legally correct term of use to accurately describe Heather's condition. In simple truth, to use a "softer" term to describe Heather's condition does not accurately describe it, and often leads people to assume things about Heather that lead to misunderstandings.

Another fact Lorraine seemed to keep missing, or chose not to acknowledge, was the clear strain keeping a retarded child at home placed on the entire family. Husbands, wives, siblings, all seemed to be worn down by the responsibility they bore. Uniformly, the parents we knew in this situation appeared to be exhausted. Many of the siblings expressed hostility or indifference to the retarded member of the family. The hostility or indifference was manifested in confrontations with the parents and, in some cases, with the retarded sibling.

When I talked to siblings of handicapped persons we knew, they almost universally told me that it was unfair to keep the handicapped person in his or her home. Some said it was unfair to them, the brothers and sisters. Most said the parents were assuming an onerous and unrealistic burden—unrealistic in the sense that they limited their own lives, and onerous in the sense that it placed physical burdens on the parents that they could not expect to meet for an extended period. Some also told me that it was also unfair to the protected child.

"What will happen when Ma and Pa go? Or if they get sick and can't take care of my brother?" one asked me, speaking of "Michael," a twenty-six-year-old cerebral palsy victim. "Michael will have to go to an institution then. None of us can take him into our homes. Not with our own families, or if we want to make a life for ourselves. An emergency placement will just kill him. I know. He should have gone to be among people like himself when he could still have adjusted to it."

Lorraine's reluctance to accept the degree of Heather's retardation was probably due to her natural optimism. Much of it was certainly due to her love for Heather. Still, I could not understand her refusal to accept what was becoming undeniable evidence.

At one point, Lorraine found a program in the Bronx that advertised spectacular success in getting several supposedly severely handicapped children to walk. Lorraine was certain this was the program we had hoped for, and I took Heather there twice. On both occasions, I was asked to leave so they could see how Heather would do without a parent around. Both times I came back and found Heather screaming loudly and, on one occasion, curled up in the fetal position. The director told me that the staff had tied her to a chair and made her stand for ten minutes. He said that she had thrown a tantrum, but they were certain they could extend her "physical abilities."

After the second visit to this program, I took Heather to Dr. Roth on a regularly scheduled visit. When he started examining Heather, Roth asked, "Has this child been sick?"

"No," I told him, "not really. Why? Is something wrong?"

"Well, she is exceptionally tight and rigid. Much more even than normal. She hasn't been having seizures, has she?"

"Seizures? No, everything is normal, except we did take her to a program that is trying to get her to stand; they say they might even be able to get her to walk or move around."

"Whatever it is that you are doing, I can only tell you that this child is dangerously tight and rigid. There is zero flex in the muscles. Hadn't you noticed that?" Roth was massaging Heather's arms and legs.

"As a matter of fact I had noticed it, and I was going to ask you if you thought this program was okay for Heather," I said, and handed Dr. Roth a brochure given to me when I enrolled Heather in the program.

Roth glanced through the brochure quickly and threw it into a wastepaper basket. "Oops, sorry," he said as he retrieved and handed it to me. "No, I don't think it is a good idea. The rigidity of your child's body is very disturbing, and I would say they are trying to get her to do something her body is not strong enough to handle. Do not go back there. Well, anyway, my advice is: do not go back there."

Heather did not go back to that program.

Two weeks after Lorraine told me that she might be pregnant, she told me she had a doctor's appointment.

"Are you going to see about the pregnancy?"

"No, I'm not pregnant. I got my period."

"When?" I asked.

"Two days ago. I'm going to see a doctor about birth control." Since Heather's birth, we had intermittently tried a foam contraceptive and condoms, both of which we found unsatisfactory. Lorraine would not take the Pill, which she said was too dangerous to a woman's health. In her medical secretary days, she had typed many test results that contained diagnoses of cancers in women who were on the Pill. She thought there was a strong connection between use of the Pill and cancer.

So the real meaning of going to see a doctor, it was clear to me, went beyond mere birth control. I needed to know what Lorraine was thinking. "Does that mean you've given up on more kids?"

I do not know if Lorraine thought the question was hostile, or merely insensitive. She may have thought I was trying to force her into choosing between Heather and my desire for more children, or she may have thought that I did not understand what a larger family could mean to Heather.

"You sound like my mother." Lorraine's tone was sharp and bitter. "Neither one of you takes care of Heather all day long. You don't know how much she needs me, how much care she needs ..."

"Lorraine," I said, raising my hand to calm her, "I'm not saying anything about Heather. I'm talking about more children."

A look of fear came over Lorraine's face again. That look was to come whenever she seemed to be feeling that she was without hope or support. This look, after a while, came to replace her looks of cheer and optimism.

"Listen, honey," she told me, "I know you want more children. I do, too. Only we can't until we know what it's going to take to care for Heather. Right now I just couldn't handle anything else. This is the only thing I can manage at this time—"

"Wait," I interrupted her, "are you saying that you think something is wrong with Heather?"

"Don't be dumb, "Lorraine said, "of course something is wrong with Heather. There's no question about it. The question is—the questions are, rather—how much is wrong and what can be done about it."

"Should we go to an attorney as Fanny suggested?"

"No!" Lorraine's shout was loud enough to frighten Heather, who started to cry. "My mother should butt the hell out. What happens is none of her business. I certainly don't see her running over here to help in any way. I think I should call her and tell—"

"All right, all right," I said, as I took Heather from her and began to rock her. She stopped crying and laughed, enjoying the movement. Lorraine's outbursts against Fanny were becoming frequent. Lorraine had expressed impatience and anger with her mother before, but lately every mention of Fanny seemed to be an expression of rancor and hostility.

"I don't know about an attorney," she said quietly. "We don't have to do it today. Let's think about it."

The period to think about going to an attorney was short. Less than a week after Lorraine had angrily talked about Fanny butting out, I came home from work to find her sitting in the kitchen in the dark. She was holding Heather in her arms, rocking her and humming softly.

I turned on the light and saw that Lorraine looked tense and defeated. Walking up to her, I put my hand on her shoulder. "What's wrong?" I asked.

"The School for the Blind won't take Heather into any of their programs." Lorraine continued to rock Heather. I said nothing, waiting for her to finish the story. She lifted Heather onto her shoulder and resumed humming. Finally she said, "They said there is no chance they can help or train her. She is too severely retarded."

"We can find others to help her, honey. We can't give up now, just because someone says 'no.'"

Lorraine sighed. "No, we won't give up. Go see the lawyer. We had better, because it looks like nobody in the world is going to help us. We are in this on our own, I guess. Balnick hurt this baby, and we should find out how. We need to find a way to help care for her."

"I will contact the lawyer first thing Monday. But what do you mean 'nobody is going to help us'? We have had help from others—"

Lorraine glanced at me and then looked away. I saw a range of emotions— anger, shame, and embarrassment—cross her face. She pursed her lips tightly, as if trying to suppress an outburst of some kind. Then she said, speaking softly, "I was walking on the boardwalk at Coney Island with Heather today. I saw Ma sitting on a bench with some of her friends. I started to walk over to talk to her, but she got a very angry look on her face and waved me away. She did not want to have to explain her granddaughter to her friends—"

"What?" I shouted. "Why, that filthy bitch—"

"No, don't get angry. It's no use. She is who she is, and she is very disappointed that her only granddaughter is handicapped—but it's clear she will be of no help to us. Not ever."

As it happens, I was riding my bike on the boardwalk a few days later and saw Fanny with a group of her friends sitting on a bench. Fanny beckoned me over, and I had a brief, but vivid, discussion of her behavior toward Heather and Lorraine. I also made certain she understood how devastating her behavior had been to Lorraine, and how it showed Fanny to be a disgusting, shallow person. Fanny started to cry and could only say, "I meant no harm." I left before she could say more, because I could feel myself only getting angrier as she tried to explain herself.

Lorraine and I are both very forgiving people, but it was many months before either of us spoke to or about her mother.

FIFTEEN

Dave Waller, my employer's house attorney, made an appointment at the "good" malpractice firm he had recommended and accompanied me to their offices on a top floor of the Pan Am Building. The date was November 16, 1970.

We sat in a wood-paneled conference room and Dave introduced me to Paul Tedesco, the "junior of the senior partners," as he called himself. Tedesco, in turn, introduced an older man, Mr. Myron Wilson, who was listed as general counsel on the firm's letterhead. Wilson said nothing during the entire meeting, only occasionally nodded sympathetically.

Tedesco started by saying that he did not want to lead me or give me clues as to what constituted malpractice. When I answered a preliminary question, he told me, I should tell the story as I knew it. The preliminary question was: had we consulted another law firm about the alleged malpractice?

"No," I told him. Dave knew most of the details, but no other attorney did, at least as far as I knew. If that answer has a quality of hedging, it's because Lorraine had a second cousin she called "Uncle Sy" who was an attorney. Fanny, who was in contact with him on a regular basis, may have asked him to look into the matter. If she had, however, she did so without the knowledge or approval of either Lorraine or myself.

"Does 'Uncle Sy' practice malpractice law?" Tedesco asked.

"I'm under the impression he practices property and estate law, but I'm not certain."

"Whatever kind of law he practices, he would be in a serious breach of ethics if he looked into the matter without your consent and knowledge," Tedesco said. "Please tell us your story."

I told of Heather's birth, her stay at University Hospital, and the reports of her current doctors.

"How old is your daughter now?"

"Nearly two."

"What kind of pregnancy did your wife have?"

"It was an easy pregnancy."

Tedesco looked over the notes he had taken. "Tell me, Mr. Zarecor," he said, "what, in your opinion, was the medical malpractice committed in this case?"

"It is clear to me—to us—that Dr. Balnick was not at the hospital until some major problem occurred in the delivery. What the problem was, how it manifested itself, or why he was not there, is not clear to us. We believe that the review of the hospital records will make those things clear, or, at least, clearer."

"On the face of it, you do seem to have a case," Tedesco said. "It's extraordinary that the doctor should not have been there, if in fact he wasn't. We'll have to obtain copies of the hospital records and have them reviewed by a doctor, just to be sure there is a case. Although getting doctors to testify against a doctor is very difficult. We'll have the initial examination of the hospital records made by an excellent man in Maryland."

"Maryland?" I asked. "Why Maryland?"

"Two reasons, primarily. First, we don't want a local doctor because he might not look closely if he knows the men and institutions involved. Second, if word gets around, he might be subject to some kind of peer pressure. The medical fraternity of New York is large, but it is also very protective of its own. They do, I guess I have to say, respond where wrong is clearly done, but it takes some pushing and prodding."

"Okay," I said. "So what do we do?"

"You will have to sign some consent forms so we can have access to the hospital records and to Balnick's records. Then I'll contact you in seven or eight weeks, when the initial examination is returned." Tedesco said. "In the meantime, take home and sign, with Lorraine, the permission forms permitting our firm access to any and all medical records. You can mail the forms back."

Tedesco handed me another two-page form. "Dave," he said, looking at Dave Waller, "have you explained to Mr. Zarecor about fees in malpractice cases?"

"No, not really," he said, speaking for the first time in the nearly two-hour meeting. "Come to think of it, I haven't even considered fees."

"We have a simple contingency fee schedule," Tedesco said, still speaking to Dave. "This gives us a sliding scale fee, standard in the business in New York State, and permitted under state law." He handed a copy of the form to Dave. "Would you like to consider it and advise your client about it?"

"Ken is not my client. I am here as a friend. This is a friendly visit. But if he asked me, I would advise him to sign it."

"I'll take my friend's advice and sign it," I laughed and signed the form. It read almost precisely as Tedesco had described it. It was the simplest legal document I have ever read.

The wheels of justice, we were to learn, turn slowly. Very slowly. Four, eight, then twelve weeks passed and we did not hear from Tedesco. Dave Waller suggested I call Tedesco, and I did. He said he was very sorry, but he was just getting around to submitting the record to the doctor in Maryland. Balnick's hospital had been slow in furnishing the records.

Another twelve weeks passed. Again, I called Tedesco, who was again sorry, but the Maryland doctor had not responded. He was certain the lack of response had nothing to do with the merits of the case. The doctor must be very busy.

Nearly a month after that conversation, we received a copy of a cover letter Tedesco was sending to the Maryland doctor. Our case, and another, was enclosed, the letter said. The doctor was urged to reply quickly. Both cases had been held up already. At the bottom of our copy of Tedesco's letter was a handwritten note:

> *I am very sorry. I cannot tell you how embarrassed I am.*
> *Please accept my assurances that you will have an answer very*
> *quickly.*

Another month passed, and a man who identified himself as Mark Billings finally called me. Paul Tedesco, he said, had left the firm to practice law in upstate New York. Billings would now be handling the case. The Maryland doctor had said we had a clear case of malpractice, and that the doctor should

71

be nailed for his handling of the delivery. The doctor had also noted that there were some "illogical and alarming" alterations to the records.

"What will happen next?"

"You and your wife will have to come down to the office so that I can meet you. You'll have to bring Heather, too, so I can see her. I'll call you when I can do it. We'll set up a mutually acceptable time."

The next call from Mark was not, however, about an appointment. He called to tell us that the majority of the firm practiced airline law, and wanted to concentrate on that. They wanted to give up the malpractice side of the business. Bill Dugan, the chief claims attorney for the firm, and the best trial attorney Mark had ever met, wanted to continue doing malpractice and claims work, however. He, along with Mark and another senior partner from the firm, was setting up the firm of Dugan Tuscano & Billings. I would be getting in the mail forms to consent to the attorneys taking our case with them to the new firm. Dugan, Tuscano & Billings is the firm that handled our case, although another firm, technically, originally accepted it.

SIXTEEN

Nearly a year passed before the firm of Dugan, Tuscano & Billings were in their new offices. We did not meet Mark face-to-face during that time, but he was active obtaining reports from the many doctors who had seen Heather. Also, the passing year made the extent of Heather's disability painfully clear. She was profoundly retarded, physically and mentally. Her right side showed more and more paralysis, and her scoliosis became pronounced as her body grew. The scoliosis, or curvature of the spine, further compromised her breathing, caused recurrent respiratory problems, and was considered dangerous by her physician. Heather started to make some movement, but not to crawl. She would only roll around. In fact, until her fourth year, we had to turn her onto her stomach before she would sleep. If we didn't turn her on her stomach, and she wanted to sleep, she would cry until she was on her stomach.

Lorraine continued to find new experts, including a nutritionist. Because Lorraine felt each and every one of these experts might be able to provide help, I dutifully went to many of these appointments or, on many occasions, took Heather by myself. None of the new specialists offered hope or, for that matter, much help. Heather was not involved with her environment, except when she was being held or played with. A noise would make her jump; loud noises made her cry. She did not respond to a call of "Heather," but would laugh or make sounds when Lorraine and I talked.

Some sounds, such as a sputtering sound, would send Heather into gales of laughter. She would laugh at the sound of Montserrat Caballe singing, but soon switched her loyalty to Dolly Parton. She would laugh whenever she heard Dolly sing and would sometimes make a humming noise when country music was played. She would also make jabbering noises when she heard Lorraine or me sing or play the piano. But her most ecstatic laughter was reserved for Dolly Parton.

Almost none of the food experiments were successful. Though we were encouraged to expand her diet, Heather flatly refused fresh fruit, except mashed banana. Eggs made her vomit. She even rejected ice cream. Lorraine, referring to the fact that I have never met any ice cream flavor I did not love and happily consume, said we might want to keep Heather's dislike of ice cream a secret. Nobody who knew me would believe any kid of mine would turn down ice cream.

In some cases the experiments with new foods were dangerous. Scrambled eggs caused a major reaction. Heather would take other foods into her mouth, and if she didn't like them, just leave them in her mouth. She had no choice; she did not know how to spit the food out, and she had not yet developed the involuntary tongue action many CP children have.

After several difficult attempts to expand her diet, we decided that Heather would have to stick with canned baby food. Attempts to get Heather to drink from a glass also met with failure. She was still drinking from a bottle on her fifth birthday.

Then there was the vicious biting phase. Heather went through a period in which any person or thing that came near her mouth was subject to a good, strong bite. Once, the doorman of our building in Manhattan innocently touched her mouth while he was saying "Hello" to her, and Heather clamped down on the poor guy's hand. Not only did she bite him, but she had to be pried loose. The doorman, who had teeth marks on his hand for days, never again made the mistake of getting a hand close to her mouth.

But it wasn't just the doorman and other people that Heather bit. Soon she was biting herself. She mutilated her left arm, and then attacked her own left thumb. We tried a number of methods to stop this impulse. Restraint, such as tying her left hand down, only succeeded in causing her to kick and cry angrily. When we finally found a solution, it was a simple one: we bought her a set of plastic keys that she could chew on instead of her own body. We were always apprehensive that Heather would break these keys in her mouth and choke on them, but she never did, and she did stop biting herself and others.

As Heather got older, the programs she attended began to close. They were victim of city, state, and federal funding cuts, all of which seemed to come simultaneously. Where Heather had been in three programs, she was soon in only one. The one remaining program was so crippled by budget cuts that the attendants could do no more than babysit the children in the program. The parents of the children got a break from caring for them, but there was little or no exercise or stimulation for the clients during the program times. Heather was nearing the age at which she was legally required to attend school, but no public school in New York could or would consider taking her as a "student."

Only United Cerebral Palsy, Inc. operated a school in Manhattan that would take Heather into their programs. The school also felt that they might even be able to expand her abilities. The difficulty was, however, that they had a four- to six-year waiting list.

We also heard of programs run by UCP in Queens that had success in training many retarded children. The Queens program, as did all good programs, had a waiting list almost as long as the school in Manhattan, and we could not even get on the list until we became residents of the borough in which the school was located.

As it happens, the lease on our tiny Manhattan apartment was expiring. Lorraine and I slept on a pullout bed in the living room, which I hated with a passion. Even though I loved Manhattan, and Lorraine loved it even more than I did, I was ready to leave that apartment. There was no privacy in it. If I wanted to listen to music and Lorraine wanted to watch television, one of us had to accede to the wishes of the other.

UCP in Brooklyn was finishing a new building that would be opened in a few months. The waiting list for the new school was only a few months long, but, as with the other programs, we could not even get onto it unless we were residents in Brooklyn. We decided to go back to Brooklyn to get Heather into the UCP program there.

After moving back to Brooklyn, however, we were told that it might be up to three years before Heather could get into the program. No explanation was offered as to why the waiting list had gone from a few months to a few years. We were only asked if we wanted to place her on the list. I told the staff that I would consider that, but I would also consider alternatives. After exploring my options, I said, I would get back to them. The fact is that I was playing a game of "chicken" with them. I did not threaten them with a lawsuit, or any other kind of pressure, but I thought maybe they would infer such from my statements, and move to find a place for Heather. That strategy did not work.

The first option I considered was suing the New York City Board of Education to demand a placement in some program for Heather. The fact is that we could not really afford a lawsuit of any kind, and I was told that suing a city agency usually turned into a very expensive proposition. I also had visions of becoming known as a person who sued at the drop of a hat. Plus while the city did lose lawsuits, the victories were often Pyrrhic—you might make your point, but the financial cost could be bankrupting. In spite of this, I made an appointment to discuss a possible lawsuit with another Manhattan law firm.

On the day set for the appointment, I was walking up Fifth Avenue in Manhattan on my way to the lawyer's office, when I met a former colleague of mine, Neil O'Brien. O'Brien and I had both worked for the City of New York in the Department of Rent and Housing Maintenance. I left that job to take more lucrative employment in the private sector, and O'Brien left to work as an assistant to a congressman from New Jersey. He also had good political connections with the Democratic Party in New York, and I had frequently helped him on campaigns he was working with after we left city employment.

"What's up, Ken?" he asked me, and added, "You have your 'serious business' face on."

I explained to him why I was in that neighborhood. When I had finished, he just shook his head. "That could take years, man. Have you talked to every possible person—like the head of UCP in New York, for example?"

"I have talked to everyone I know to talk to," I said, "but nobody seems to be able to help."

"Wait, wait just one minute." O'Brien brightened considerably. "I bet I know someone who can help you. Where are you going to be this afternoon?"

"In my office, working," I said.

"Go there and wait for a call. I know who can help you, and I need to get to a phone to call him now." O'Brien took my phone number and told me to go back to work and to wait until I heard from him.

I never did hear from O'Brien again, but at about 3:30 PM I got a call from an officious-sounding woman who asked me for my home address, phone number, and Heather's name and Social Security number. She then said, "Please stay on the line for the president."

The president? President of what? I almost hung up, but before I could, a male voice said "Hello? Are you the father of the handicapped girl?"

"Yes, I am. Her name is Heather—"3

"Can you tell me your story?" the voice asked.

"Sure," I responded, "but first can I ask, who are you?"

The man laughed. "I'm sorry. I thought you were told. I am Salvatore Macri, the president of the borough of Brooklyn. It's a little elective job we have here in New York."

Suddenly this picture was becoming clearer to me. I gave Macri a quick summary of Heather's story and what UCP had told us about placing her in their program.

After I finished, there was a pause. "Well," Macri said, "I don't see that this is a problem at all. I think I can help."

"We would be eternally grateful, sir."

"It is nothing—I guess that is what we are supposed to do. Nice when we can actually do something. Well," Macri said, "I'm not sure it can get done today, but someone should be contacting you in a day or two."

The next day around noon, I got a call from UCP in Brooklyn. They had found a place for Heather in their program, and she could start as soon as busing could be arranged. Could I, or my wife, come to the school the following Monday to arrange everything? Lorraine kept that appointment, and Heather was in the Brooklyn program in a few weeks.

I had worked on several political campaigns, but this was the first time any political influence was used on my, or my family's, behalf. Using political connections was not an option I had considered until the chance encounter with O'Brien, and I have often wondered how long it would have been before Heather was in a program if that meeting had never happened. O'Brien and Macri committed a gratuitous act of kindness, as one of my friends would say, in helping us. We were both deeply grateful for it, but I could not help but wonder about others we knew in the same situation that did not have access to such help. There was no question of feeling guilty about accepting this help—I never did—still, there are many who could use such kindness, too, but never come close to getting it.

SEVENTEEN

Lorraine was forty pounds heavier than she had been at the time of Heather's birth by 1973. She was carrying about 185 pounds on a five-foot frame. I could see she was having problems handling Heather, and the added weight was causing health problems. I began to wonder how much longer she would be able to cope with handling Heather physically.

Clearer in my mind was the virtual certainty that Heather would never be able to do one thing for herself. It was time, it seemed to me, to see what alternatives were available to us.

Lorraine would not discuss institutionalizing Heather, but I did not see how we could escape it. Institutionalization should happen soon, if it were going to. I thought the longer we waited, the harder it would be for Lorraine, and if we waited much longer, I might not only lose a daughter, but a wife as well.

About this time, Geraldo Rivera of WABC news in New York was doing a series of television reports on New York State institutions for the retarded. He had started at Willowbrook on Staten Island. His reports showed appalling conditions; conditions one simply did not want to believe could exist in this supposedly most "liberal" state in the union. Each attendant at Willowbrook, who made a salary barely above the minimum wage, had to care for between thirty and forty residents. Six or seven patients are the most one attendant could properly handle.

Residents lived in their own filth, usually unclothed. They were heavily sedated. Many showed signs of physical abuse—scratches, bruises, and open wounds.

The news got only more appalling: the fact is that Willowbrook may not have been the worst facility for the retarded in the state of New York. Incredibly, the fact was that these conditions, for all their shock value when they appeared on a television screen, were widely known generally, and were well known in the mental health community. Among professionals in the state government, the conditions were a matter of common knowledge. That did not prevent officials of the state from firing the two staff members who had informed Rivera of the situation at Willowbrook. The point of all that seemed to me to be that nobody in state government considered the care and treatment of totally helpless people worth any amount of time or attention, and that they also were in no mood to have a public discussion of the matter.

After Rivera started his series, the stories were on many television news programs in New York. Both Lorraine and I finally got to a point where we would simply change the channel whenever another example of the abuse of the retarded appeared. One night, however, I was only half-watching the news, when I saw Rivera come onto the screen. What he was saying stopped me before I could change the channel: he had found some file footage, he said, showing Robert Kennedy, who represented New York in the United States Senate at the time, talking to reporters after an inspection of Willowbrook. Kennedy appeared to be traumatized by what he had just seen. He was saying the conditions in the facility were appalling, degrading, and inhuman, and he called for sweeping, immediate changes to improve conditions there. Rivera had one more shocking detail: this file footage was from September 9, 1965. In other words, these conditions existed for years before Rivera started his reports, and, in spite of what was happening to clients at Willowbrook, nothing had been done to end the neglect and maltreatment.

I began to understand and agree with Lorraine's statements that she would rather die than see Heather go into a public institution in New York State. That did not alter the fact, however, that the time was getting closer when we might be forced to deal with a placement in an institution out of a true need to do so. We could not and, at this point, would not consider placing Heather in a public institution, but I was afraid we might be placed in an untenable position if Lorraine became unable to cope with her physically. So I searched for alternatives so that we could choose when and how we would act, rather than wait and be forced to act from a point of defeat and desperation.

As far as I could see, we had three alternatives besides public institutions:

the first was just to continue what we were doing. This, obviously, was the preferred option of Lorraine, but again I was not convinced it was the realistic alternative. Second, neighboring states, such as Connecticut, did not seem to have the problems New York had with public institutions for the retarded. In fact, Connecticut had an excellent reputation for the care it gave to its handicapped population. We could move there. Or, third, we could use a private institution, assuming we could find one and could afford it.

Lorraine and I agreed we should consider going to Connecticut. I began looking for a job there and sent Lorraine there, mostly to Stamford, to look for housing. She went mostly on weekends.

The northeast was experiencing an economic decline at this time. It was difficult finding jobs in Connecticut, and none I found paid nearly enough to justify a move there, let alone support us and pay for the expensive care for Heather.

Lorraine enjoyed the trips but pointed out moving to Connecticut would mean that she would be unable to see her mother much. I sincerely did not understand why that would be a problem, and I am not certain Lorraine was all that worried about it, either. She did keep detailing, however, problems with the houses and apartments she saw. The three of us were living at that time in a dark, one-bedroom apartment in Manhattan, but she felt this was much better than anything she had seen in Stamford or in any of the other places she had been. She also hated the idea of my commuting to work and her commuting to her school. She said it would cut down on our time together. Somehow, Lorraine could not accept the idea that people work or go to school in Connecticut as well as in New York City.

Lorraine also made the point frequently that she thought expecting her to work was unfair. She had as much as she could be expected to handle just caring for Heather, going to school, and working a single day at a hospital typing biopsy reports. Going to Hunter College was a great joy for Lorraine, and it was her main escape from the house. She was studying art history. When I teased her that this was certainly the field to go into if you wanted an in-demand job skill, she said she would find some sugar daddy to support her. "I won't look for my new sugar daddy from Nebraska," she told me, "all the guys from there that I know seem to be very cheap."

Economic considerations eventually dictated that we would have to stay in the state of New York.

The alternative of placing Heather in a private institution remained. Without Lorraine's knowledge, I contacted six private institutions. I got their names and addresses from an association for the retarded whose program Heather attended, and got references from other sources. Four of these places were eliminated: two would not even consider taking Heather based on her medical history; two were rejected without even submitting a medical history because of the bad references I received. In the end, I only visited one institution.

The costs were prohibitive in all the places I contacted. In 1974, the least expensive institution cost nearly $18,000 a year. "Extras," such as nursing care in case the client became ill, laundry expenses if the laundry was not done at home, special diets, physical therapy, etc., were additional at most of them.

In 1974, that was pretty much our net income, so it was clear there was no way we could afford to pay for a placement ourselves and still provide our own food and shelter. The state of New York, however, had a program for aiding parents who institutionalized retarded children in private institutions. They were supposedly paying to send many handicapped children to private institutions out of state. I started research to determine if this was, in fact, a possibility.

Our conversations about Lorraine returning to work became very tense. "What do you suggest we do with Heather?" she would demand.

"We could hire a babysitter, or we could send her away during the week and bring her home on the weekends."

"Only her mother can take care of her. No babysitter understands how to properly respond to her and fulfill her needs. I have to do it. Only I can do it." Lorraine gave me a long, careful look. "Surely you are not considering letting the state care for Heather after what we have seen on television. That is unthinkable …"

"New York State does not run every facility in the world for retarded children."

"They are all as bad or worse. Every child's place is in a home with a mother and a father."

"That's true, but children also grow up and leave home, sooner or later. The difference is, in our case Heather will leave home at an earlier age. When we can no longer handle her."

"We can still handle her. At least I can, anyway." Lorraine began gesturing frantically, and shifting back and forth on her feet, as she did often when she felt pressured, or became angry. "We don't have to think about anything this drastic for many, many more years, if ever."

"It is not going to be easier to do in a year, two years or whenever ..." I broke off. We had been around these circles several times, and I doubted that Lorraine heard a thing I was saying. Of course, she would probably say that I had stopped listening, too, since by this point each of us was only repeating statements made before.

I tried another approach. "We were talking about your going back to work full-time."

"Well, we're going to end this discussion. I can't. I am a mother, a nearly full-time student, and a housewife. Each of these occupations is full-time. I could not possibly work. You are the family breadwinner, such as it is. I don't have to work; it is your duty to provide for Heather and me, Ma says. She also says that I should not let you shame me into abandoning Heather."

In point of fact, all my planning and scheming to be able to afford an institution for Heather was pointless. A friend who worked for the state government did some checking for me, and told me New York State was no longer giving aid for parents to institutionalize handicapped children in private institutions. The funds simply were not available.

More than the fact of New York State having no money to pay for the program, the institutions I contacted responded unanimously that they could not accept a child as severely retarded as Heather. (The phrase usually used was "her involvement is too great.") They were very sorry.

Of the six institutions on my list, one of the two remaining, a place in Florida, did inform me that, after reviewing the records they had received, they were pleased to inform us that they would consider taking Heather in case of some unspecified "emergency." The fee schedule, however, would have to be "adjusted" to include supplemental nursing care.

I was mildly encouraged by this. It was the first positive response after a long search. The response was somewhat vague, and before I could ask for clarification, it became clear that this place would never do. Less than a week after getting the letter, I noticed a short item on the back pages of the *New York Times,* which reported a lawsuit against the place alleging maltreatment of its clients. New York State, surely the pariah of the entire nation in care for the handicapped, was instituting the suit. I could not, nor would even care to, imagine how bad conditions were if New York felt that something had to be done to correct them.

Lorraine did not know that I was in contact with anyone concerning institutionalizing Heather. She did not even know that I took a day off and visited one of the places I had contacted in Pennsylvania.

I arrived at the Rose Home for the Retarded and Handicapped outside of Philadelphia shortly before noon for a 12:30 PM appointment. Using the available time, I walked around the "campus." The buildings were old, brick, and most were a single story high. There was a lot of sidewalk. Most of the sidewalks had a rail on one or both sides. All of the large lawns were well tended, as were the flowers. A closer look at the flowers revealed they were mostly plastic, which explained why daffodils were blooming in October.

Near a building marked CLASSROOMS, I heard a piano playing. The piano was accompanying a cacophony of laughter, unspecific vocal sounds, and chatter. A raised voice brought the noise to a stop. The voice enunciated the words of the song carefully. When the piano started again, the noise resumed as before.

At 12:30 PM, I presented myself at the administration building. A Mrs. Shirley Cohen introduced herself. She was the staff psychologist and was to be my guide. Mrs. Cohen was extremely nervous. She smoked incessantly. As she spoke, her eyes would dart around. When she was sitting and not talking, her right foot was bouncing up and down. When I was talking, she absentmindedly rattled paper or fanned herself with it, although it was not warm in her office.

Mrs. Cohen asked several questions about Heather and how we were managing her care at home. She took a medical history, even though I had submitted copies of many of the medical reports we had gotten. She was not surprised when I said Lorraine did not know I was visiting Rose.

"You are considering a very important step," she said, "one that has literally destroyed families. I can appreciate your wanting to cover the ground first, so to speak, before taking your wife over it. But it's not a good idea for one party to do this on his own. Since I don't know your wife, however, I guess I have no idea how she will respond."

The patients at Rose that I saw appeared to be at least teenagers or adults. They were all being kept busy. In a large recreation room, two large men were trying to pedal adult-sized tricycles. Both men had trouble coordinating their movements, but they kept trying. An instructor offered constant encouragement to all the people in the room. Several were playing with a beach ball. No matter what their ages, all squealed happily as they chased the ball. Whenever one of the players picked up the ball, the others stood aside, letting the handler take all the time needed to throw or kick it. None of them could really handle the beach ball, but they all seemed to be having a great time trying.

In another classroom, several residents were knitting and sewing. The program has been started with some apprehension, Mrs. Cohen told me, because the staff was not certain any of the residents could manage needles and other sharp objects. After two months, the results were gratifying. "We train our clients," she said, "every day they are here. Our goals may have to be small, but we keep trying."

As we went from building to building, Mrs. Cohen said, "We have a rigidly enforced male-female segregation here. We only have female nurses on the female dorms, and we never allow the male and female clients to be together without supervision."

I suppose just a little thought would have made clear to me why this segregation was necessary, but I asked, "Why?"

"These men and women have normal sex drives and normal bodies for it. Well, many or even most of them do. What they don't have, of course, is the normal capacity to control their urges or to express them. Pregnancies among retarded women have not been uncommon. Not here, let me say, it hasn't happened here—because we keep socialization among the clients rigidly controlled. Unhappily, normal men—guards or ward attendants—have made some of the pregnancies. We have been very successful in preventing this kind of tragedy, too."

Nausea overtook me, but I continued following Mrs. Cohen into the next building. It was marked HOSPITAL BUILDING—AUTHORIZED PERSONNEL ONLY. It was, as were all the other buildings that I had been shown, neat, clean, and had a powerful smell of disinfectant.

Four hospital beds lined the wall of the main ward. There was a thin, small figure on one of the beds. At the sound of our voices, the figure made a gurgling sound and began making a waving motion.

"Hello, Louisa," Mrs. Cohen said. Louisa's arms seemed pinned to her sides. Her hands were crossed at chest level. It appeared Louisa could only raise her hands a couple of inches, but she was smiling and waving enthusiastically.

"This is Mr. Zarecor, Louisa. He came to see your home." Mrs. Cohen turned her back to Louisa and put her hand to her mouth. Recovering quickly, she turned back to the child and asked, "How are you today, Louisa? Do you feel better?"

Louisa smiled, gurgled, and continued to wave.

I looked at Mrs. Cohen and Louisa. "Doesn't she want to be held?" I asked.

"Yes, yes, please," Mrs. Cohen said. "Pick her up if you want. We try to encourage handling around here."

Uncertain, I picked Louisa up and cradled her in my arms. She gave a giggle and rested her head on my chest. I looked questioningly at Mrs. Cohen.

"Her parents placed her here about three years ago. Louisa was a late baby, and both parents have medical problems of their own. They could not handle her anymore. They have not been back once, as far as I know. When Louisa came, she could walk, play, and she had a vocabulary of twenty or thirty words. Since coming, she gradually lost all those abilities."

Louisa was making a soft crooning sound. "She is very content," Mrs. Cohen was smiling, too, for the first time.

"How old is Louisa?" I asked.

"Twelve, nearly thirteen." Louisa could not have weighed more than thirty pounds and was no more than three feet tall.

"What's wrong—what happened to her?" I asked, and was sorry I had asked the question the second the words were spoken. Mrs. Cohen bit her lip and again turned her back on us.

"All of these children have respiratory problems, and Louisa's are increasingly severe. Children like Louisa, in the best of institutions—which we may be—have other problems. I have seen institutionalized children of all ages who seem to be doing all right and then simply die for no identifiable cause. I have read—it is in the literature about institutionalized children—that they often die simply because they are not touched, because they feel no warmth or love. I think that is what is happening here." Mrs. Cohen turned back to us, obviously struggling to maintain her composure. She wiped her eyes and continued. "Louisa is dying, I would say, because she has lost the love she had in her home."

Mrs. Cohen blew her nose, took a deep breath, and seemed to regain control of her emotions.

"She has gone to sleep in your arms. Lay her down, and we'll go have some tea or coffee in the cafeteria."

We inspected the cafeteria but went back to Mrs. Cohen's office to drink our coffee. She laced her own with some bourbon, which I declined.

"I am very sorry, Mr. Zarecor. I really should not be doing this job, I guess."

"If I can ask an impertinent but obvious question, why are you?"

"I am committed to good care for the handicapped. And I have a brother and a daughter here."

About a week later, Mrs. Cohen called me at my job to give me the by-now expected statement that Heather was too severely retarded to be admitted to any program at Rose. The facility was simply not equipped to handle her.

I thanked her for her help and the tour. "By the way," I asked, "how is Louisa?"

"She died yesterday, Mr. Zarecor."

"I am sorry," I said. "I am very sorry."

"Her family came and claimed the body today. At least she will be able to rest among them."

"Yes," I agreed, "but it is still very sad."

"You are a kind man, Mr. Zarecor. I hope life goes well for you, your wife, and Heather. Good-bye."

"I wish the same to you. Good-bye, Mrs. Cohen."

EIGHTEEN

Lorraine and I finally met Mark Billings in mid-1972. We were surprised to find ourselves shaking hands with a giant (six-foot-six or -seven) man, who appeared to be as broad as he was tall. Standing by himself, he appeared to be bigger than Lorraine and I did together. We laughed about that as we took our seats in Mark's cramped Manhattan office. Lorraine became increasingly uncomfortable during the discussion. Whenever Mark or I were speaking, she would carry on a running commentary under her breath. We frequently stopped to ask her what she was saying. She, in turn, would just shake her head and say, "Nothing, nothing. Go on with your conversation."

"First," Mark told us, "we need to go over the list of all the doctors that have examined Heather, all of her therapy groups, and all the expenses involved. Is Heather receiving physical therapy at this time?"

I started to answer him, but Lorraine blurted out, "I don't like it. The baby cries whenever she goes. I have to take her in her little stroller on the subway. Sometimes I get help, sometimes I don't."

"So I can assume she is getting physical therapy, then?"

"When I take her, I go to bad neighborhoods. People do sometimes help me up and down the subway stairs, as I said. A lot of people tell me they don't know how I do it, carrying her around like that …"

"The answer is 'yes,'" I interrupted. "She's getting therapy at one hospital in Brooklyn and is in one therapy program here in Manhattan."

"They send a bus for us to go to the one in Manhattan, even though it is not too far," Lorraine said, "but we take the subway to the Brooklyn one. That's in the bad neighborhood."

The interview continued on like this for about an hour. Mark continued questioning us patiently. He would frequently have to lead Lorraine back to the question to get a direct answer. When I answered a question, she would interject that caring for Heather was a burden, most of which she had to bear. Initially, I was angry at Lorraine for insisting on going around the questions, and I began to resent her implication that only she took care of Heather. Soon, however, I realized she was avoiding a direct acknowledgment of Heather's retardation, even while seeking some sort of validation for all her efforts. Here I was somewhat lost—how could I provide that validation beyond what I was doing already? There was no question that I was involved in Heather's care—I, for example, always fed Heather lunch and supper if I was home, took her for walks, bathed her, and included her in most of the activities I undertook while at home. Lorraine and I also did many things together, such as going to movies, theater, and, of course, the opera.

The realization came to me that Lorraine was not relating to the world as it existed. She appeared to be unable to say to Mark, or to anyone, in so many words, "Yes, Heather is a retarded child." Lorraine was living with the problem every hour of the day, and she was taking Heather to places that offered only slight hope. The people who ran those programs did not hesitate to point out frequently that their program may be good for Heather, but we should understand there would never be any kind of dramatic improvement. A straightforward acknowledgment that Heather would never lead a "normal" life, it seemed to me, would make life simpler, but Lorraine's choice was to try to cope without that admission. Many people I know live with half-truth rationalizations to justify beliefs and behavior, but this faulty thinking in the end undermines or outright destroys relationships and usually hinders true progress in the situation at hand.

Mark, after getting more information from both of us, told us that the next step in the process would be to hold an examination before trial (or EBT). This would allow attorneys for Dr. Balnick and the hospital to question us. More important, Mark could question Balnick. The hospital would also have to produce the original birth record. Working with a photocopy, Mark had to guess at many of the words. Some entries appeared to be crossed out and marked over; others seemed to begin in one handwriting and end in another. He said he was very anxious to see the original record. The examination before trial could, he hoped, take place soon.

By the time the lawsuit was filed, we were back in Brooklyn, so it was filed in the Kings County Supreme Court. The suit brought complaints against the hospital, four doctors on the hospital staff, and, of course, Balnick.

The pretrial examinations were scheduled but postponed at the request of the attorney representing Balnick. The malpractice insurance carriers hired the attorneys for Balnick, the other doctors named in our complaint, and the hospital. None of the parties in the suit hired an attorney themselves, and they did not even have approval over the attorneys hired to represent them at trial.

We ran through seven postponements and an awesome array of excuses before the pretrial examinations were finally held. They were held August 19, 1975, which was just three months short of the fifth anniversary of my interview with Paul Tedesco that had initiated the suit.

The examinations were scheduled for 10:00 AM, in the offices of Dugan, Tuscano & Billings. In addition to Mark, two other attorneys were present: Paul White, representing Balnick, and Joseph DeSapio, representing the hospital. The other four doctors we were suing were not scheduled to be examined. White and DeSapio would represent their interest, should an issue come up. Balnick, Lorraine, the librarian from the hospital, and I were scheduled to testify in the morning.

We arrived before ten, giving us time to talk to Mark. Balnick was already in the conference room when we arrived, going over records with Paul White. Incredibly, he smiled and waved at Lorraine when he saw her. She did not return the greeting, partly because, she later said, she did not recognize him when she first saw him.

Mark was very cheerful and asked if we had any questions. We had none, and he had none for us. We should listen to the questions, Mark said, wait to hear if he made an objection, and if there was no objection, answer in as few words as possible. Most important, he repeated, answer only what is asked. Do not give them material to use, or ask questions of the other side.

The librarian was the first to testify. Her function was to deliver the hospital record, to say this was the record, and to wait while it was being used. Mark held the document up so we all could see it.

MARK: Is this the entire record?

LIBRARIAN: Yes. To the best of my knowledge it is. The

hospital was asked to show this record to several parties. But I'm certain it's the entire record.

MARK: There is no X-ray with the record. Has there ever been an X-ray with it? The record states that Mrs. Zarecor was taken to the X-ray room.

LIBRARIAN: I can't be certain. I've been handling the record for several years, and I've never seen one.

MARK: Could you search for it?

PAUL WHITE: Do you know for certain there was an X-ray? Maybe one was never taken.

MARK: An examination of the hospital record would reveal several references to it.

LIBRARIAN: A thorough search is always made whenever a record is subpoenaed. But I'll institute another.

Lorraine was questioned next. White began by questioning her about her first contact with Balnick, talking her through going to Planned Parenthood before our marriage. She went to obtain birth control methods and dilation, she said. Planned Parenthood had referred her to Balnick. The doctors on her job knew Balnick, or knew of him, and they concurred that he was an excellent man.

White did not go into the subject, but Lorraine had been a virgin when I met her. Sex had been difficult until the dilation.

After the initial appointments, we both went to see Balnick. He took the required blood samples when we got our marriage license. Lorraine said the next time she went to Balnick was for medical care during her pregnancy.

Mark led Lorraine through the pregnancy, which Lorraine said was very easy. She did not remember any problems.

When White started to question Lorraine, he abruptly changed the line of questioning:

WHITE: Do you have any brothers or sisters?

LORRAINE: One brother.

Mark asked if he might say something off the record. The other attorneys agreed. White's anticipated line of questioning, Mark said, was out of order or at least premature. Nothing had been said to establish Heather had problems, no matter what the cause. He would, however, allow Lorraine to answer.

WHITE: What does your brother do for a living?

LORRAINE: He's a messenger.

WHITE: For a company?

LORRAINE: Yes.

WHITE: Do you know the name of the company?

LORRAINE: No, I don't.

Mark looked over to me and nodded. We all knew where this line of questioning was headed. White knew, from medical histories we gave to every new doctor or group Heather was taken to, that Lenny, Lorraine's brother, had been hospitalized with a nervous breakdown. He, in turn, gave all medical records submitted by us to all the defendants. Mark knew, and had told us to expect, that the defendants would try to link Heather's retardation to a congenital cause. Exactly how such a connection could be made between her retardation and a nervous breakdown escaped both Mark and us.

White continued questioning Lorraine about her family:

WHITE: Did your brother graduate from high school?

LORRAINE: Yes.

(Lorraine gave White an angry look. His line of questioning was helping her conquer the fear she felt before the questioning began.)

WHITE: Do you have any other brothers or sisters who are not living?

LORRAINE: No.

WHITE: To your own knowledge, did your mother have any miscarriages?

LORRAINE: No.

WHITE: You know she did not, or you don't remember?

LORRAINE: No, she did not.

White paused and then, without any preface, changed the line of questioning again:

WHITE: What do you remember about the delivery?

LORRAINE: Very little. I remember being taken to the X-ray room and being talked to by the nurses. I remember the nurses tell me not to press down.

WHITE: To the best of your recollection, no doctors, Balnick or otherwise, examined you from the time you were admitted until just before the operation?

LORRAINE: Yes. Only nurses examined me, as I remember it. I remember clearly being awake for the operation.

Again, White abruptly switched gears:

WHITE: Tell me about current medical costs.

LORRAINE: My husband paid all these bills. He almost never talks to me about them.

This was true. We used the same checkbook, and Lorraine could see any entry made in it, and she usually opened the mail when bills were sent to us, but she never seemed to pay attention to them. The cost of sending Heather to all of those doctors and groups was not minor, but it was also not unbearable. Insurance, which I got through my employers, paid many of the charges. Our concern, in any case, was for future costs.

White closed his questioning of Lorraine, asking about Heather's current care. As she had done to Mark in our private meeting, Lorraine usually evaded giving direct answers to questions.

WHITE: Are there any costs that you are incurring at this moment—that is, ongoing costs other than the ones you have testified to, costs relating to her care at home now?

LORRAINE: Well, I would like to explain …

MARK: What my client wants to say is that, while expenses to date have been large, anticipated expenses are much greater.

WHITE: No. I'm not willing to agree. I don't understand how …

DESAPIO: Come on, Paul.

This is the first time DeSapio spoke, and it caught us all by surprise.

DESAPIO: If the kid is not ambulatory, if she has no use of her limbs, and if she's blind—

WHITE: She's blind?

MARK: Yes. It's in the records we've submitted to you. It's in two or three of the reports.

DESAPIO: Anyway, if the kid is all of these things, she can do nothing for herself—

At this point, DeSapio and White exchanged hostile looks. I very nearly asked White if he went to all of his pretrial depositions unprepared, but held my peace.

WHITE: Is she toilet trained?

LORRAINE: No.

I now spoke for the first time, since we were still off the record:

KENNETH: Obviously. In her present condition, toilet training Heather is out of the question.

DESAPIO: You mean that at the age of five or six—how old is she? Six? Yes, at the age of six, she is still in diapers?

KENNETH: Yes.

DeSapio's eyes widened as if in surprise, and he shook his head. White looked very annoyed, and his annoyance only increased as DeSapio continued:

DESAPIO: Anyway, what they're trying to say is that she—the kid, I mean—will need more and more help, as she gets older and larger.

White had a fixed, exasperated grin on his face and turned red. He scowled at DeSapio. DeSapio waved his hand, shrugged, and suggested letting the questioning continue. As we went back on record, Lorraine tried to complete her answer:

LORRAINE: We could use—

WHITE: The question was: are there any ongoing costs at the present time that you have not testified to?

LORRAINE: No.

White knew that we had a nurse's aide to take care of Heather while Lorraine attended class at Hunter College. He tried to get her to say so.

WHITE: Have you ever paid any individual to help you in the care of your child?

A woman named Claire, who was a certified nurse's aide, did take care of Heather while Lorraine went to her college classes.

LORRAINE: Is Claire considered—?

WHITE: Did you pay an individual?

LORRAINE: We paid someone—an aide. But this aide was afraid to go home at night. I had to pay her cab fare home. She—

WHITE: That's fine, Mrs. Zarecor. No further questions.

DeSapio had no questions for Lorraine, and Mark suggested that they might be able to question me before the lunch break. Questioning Lorraine, even with all the interruptions and run-arounds, had taken just one hour, from 10:45 AM to 11:45 AM. Everyone agreed to try to get my examination done.

White immediately got to the possibility of a congenital reason for Heather's retardation. This contention seemed to be the defense's highest card:

WHITE: Do you have any brothers or sisters?

KENNETH: I have eight brothers and four sisters.

WHITE: Did your mother, to your knowledge, have any miscarriages or stillborn children?

KENNETH: She had none.

WHITE: Do you know if any of your brothers or sisters, to your knowledge, have what we term a learning disability of any type?

Mark made a pro forma objection to the question, but he said I could answer it if I knew. I thought the question was ludicrous. Like most families of all sizes that I know, we have our share of overachievers, underachievers, and those who do just enough to get by. My family is, however, a bunch of conservative Republicans that had—or has, more accurately—yet to forgive Franklin Roosevelt for starting this country on the perilous road to socialism. It occurred to me to say that my family's politics was the only learning disability I could think of. Instead I said, "None. There are no learning disabilities among my brothers and sisters, and no physical disabilities, either."

Finally, White asked me about institutionalizing Heather, specifically about state-operated institutions.

> KENNETH: Well, the truth of the matter is that I, largely without my wife's knowledge, have looked into institutionalizing the child.
>
> WHITE: What have been the results of that investigation?
>
> KENNETH: Absolutely disastrous for state-sponsored schools because they are inhuman—absolutely unacceptable, private or public …

I saw Lorraine, who had just learned that I had looked into institutions for Heather, was breaking down and starting to cry. Reaching over to her, I took her in my arms and comforted her.

White, looking at a loss and somewhat upset, said quietly, "I understand."

White had no more questions, and DeSapio had none. We took a break for lunch. We went out for a quick bite at a deli. Lorraine was calm. She wondered if White had bothered to even meet Balnick before this morning. She never brought up my checking out institutions for Heather. Mark said we had both done well, and we should all be pleased. Balnick was to testify next. Mark was anxious for that.

Though she was feeling better, Lorraine asked to be excused from the afternoon session. She was not up, she said, to listening to Balnick lie and evade. I intended to stay for all of it, because I was as anxious as Mark was to hear what Balnick would say.

Balnick was again waiting in the conference room when we returned from lunch. It was amazing to me to see he was still wearing the same old gray suit he was wearing seven years ago when I first met him. He had worn that suit—it looked to be the same suit to me, anyway—every time I saw him.

As the session started, Paul White said he hoped it would not last more than two hours, as he had a 4:30 train to catch.

MARK: Dr. Balnick, would you please describe your medical training and the meaning of medical specialty certification?

BALNICK: I am a board-certified, a diplomat of the American Board of Physicians in Obstetrics and Gynecology. I ...

Balnick seemed willing, even eager, to answer Mark's questions, but White kept objecting. Discussions were held, at length, off the record, concerning the pertinence of the questions about Balnick's credentials.

White finally acceded, allowing Mark to again ask what "board certification" meant, exactly. "Well, this is the ..." Balnick started, assuming, as I had, that there was agreement on allowing such questions. White, however, raised his hand for Balnick to stop. First he said, "I won't let him answer that because I'm not too enthralled with it." DeSapio started to say something, but White made a face and waved him off as he said to Balnick, "Go ahead and answer."

BALNICK: This is the highest form of recognition for proficiency in a special field.

MARK: How many medical societies did you hold memberships in, in 1969?

BALNICK: Six. (He listed them.)

MARK: And did you receive the journals from these various organizations?

BALNICK: I did.

MARK: And do you consider yourself current in reading the journals?

BALNICK: Yes. I'm well informed of the "improvements" in the state of the art.

MARK: Doctor, did there come a time when Lorraine Zarecor came to your attention for treatment?

Balnick pulled his office records from an envelope. Mark had never seen them and immediately asked for a copy. Copies were made for him and DeSapio. The copies were marked by the court reporter.

BALNICK: In response to your question, I found, on examination,

Mrs. Zarecor to be a virgin. We did a hymeneal dilation—a stretch of the hymen—to make intercourse feasible.

MARK: Anything else?

BALNICK: On later visits, I prescribed the Pill, but I understand she would not take it.

Attention turned to Balnick's office records. Mark, leafing through the copy given to him, asked if it was the complete record. The pagination was unclear; pages seemed to be missing. "Does that," Mark asked, indicating Balnick's copy, "purport to be a complete copy of your original office records?"

Glancing at the copy Balnick and White were sharing, Mark realized they were also looking at a photocopy of the record. He asked if the original of the record still existed.

White again answered for his client. "I believe so."

Mark and Balnick went through the pregnancy, discussing every visit from August 8, 1968, the day Lorraine went to find out if she was pregnant, until the delivery.

MARK: Would you agree with the earlier testimony that the pregnancy was "easy"?

BALNICK: I would agree the pregnancy was easy. Lorraine had a cold at the end, which was not serious and no problem to the pregnancy. She was, however, overweight at the start of the pregnancy and gained too much weight during it.

Balnick seemed to have found a theme. He referred to her heaviness eleven times in the course of the afternoon.

MARK: Please describe the prenatal care.

BALNICK: I gave standard, good prenatal care. All the signs were good. No problems. A part of the "good" obstetric care was a vaginal examination at every visit. When you do a vaginal examination on a pregnant woman, you automatically measure once, and you evaluate the pelvis. You try to figure the contour of the bony pelvis.

MARK: How had you heard Lorraine was in the hospital?

BALNICK: It was a routine message that every private patient—

Paul White interrupted Balnick. The interruptions were to become increasingly common. "He wants to know what the message was," White told his client. Balnick looked carefully at White, as if trying to ascertain what White was trying to do. The look was also not too friendly.

BALNICK (quoting another doctor): "Your patient is admitted. I examined her. She was prepared, and she is not doing much. She is not doing anything."

MARK: When you say "not doing anything", what does that mean to you as a doctor?

BALNICK: That means she is not in labor.

Mark turned from Balnick's office records to the hospital record. As he had suspected, the original hospital record contained several entries that had been crossed out with heavy black ink. Other entries were simply written over.

Balnick said the hospital record showed he had examined Lorraine at 3:30 PM, on March 27.

MARK: This was your first examination?

BALNICK: Yes, sir, it was.

MARK: That was nearly sixteen hours after Mrs. Zarecor was admitted, isn't that correct?

BALNICK: Yes, I guess it was. But—

WHITE: Wait for a question, Doctor.

BALNICK: All right. Yes.

MARK: How far is your office from the hospital, Doctor?

BALNICK: About five minutes by cab, twelve to fifteen minutes walking.

As I watched Balnick, it seemed to me that he did not find any significance in the questions, or in his answers. He appeared to be relaxed and he was smiling. Mark and Balnick went through every single entry in the hospital record in detail. White continued making additions to Balnick's answers, and continued to try to stop or direct answers. He did so much talking, in fact, that I was beginning to wonder whose testimony was being taken here.

> MARK: Dr. Balnick, the hospital examination record, which indicates Lorraine was not near delivery at 3:30 PM, has what appears to be your signature and another signature.
>
> BALNICK: I … yes … I … well, the resident had signed it and I signed his name "to endorse the finding as checked by me." The examination was done at 3:30 in the afternoon.
>
> MARK: When did you next see Mrs. Zarecor?
>
> BALNICK: That woman must have been examined every hour.
>
> MARK: Would these examinations normally be contained in the hospital records?

White again held up his hands, indicating that Balnick should hold his answer.

> WHITE: What do you mean by "normally"?
>
> MARK: Would the normal procedure of the hospital and your procedure, Doctor, be to put in the labor chart, labor sheet, every examination of the patient that you would make?
>
> BALNICK: They should be.
>
> MARK: According to the record you have in your hand, Doctor, when was the next examination?
>
> BALNICK: The next examination recorded here is at 7:00 PM.
>
> MARK: Were you present for this examination, Doctor?
>
> BALNICK: Yes. I was.
>
> MARK: Look at the "Examiner" column, Doctor, please. Did you sign there?
>
> BALNICK: Yes, I signed it, over the name of the intern.

One single item in the record was unmistakably in Balnick's handwriting. It was his request for approval to perform a Caesarean. Under the rules of the hospital, no Caesarean was to be performed without the approval of two doctors—the senior resident on duty and the operating physician.

Under further questioning, Balnick told Mark that after Lorraine had been in the hospital for several hours, he ordered an X-ray taken of her pelvis.

> MARK: Did you ever read those X-rays yourself, or see them?
>
> BALNICK: At 3:30, sir.
>
> MARK: What did you observe in looking at the X-rays yourself?
>
> BALNICK: There was no cephalopelvic disproportion.
>
> MARK: In layman's terms, Doctor, that means what?
>
> BALNICK: The pelvic structure was adequate and the baby was fairly small, therefore, as far as mechanical impediment to the birth, there would not be any.

More cross-outs were gone over. Balnick could not say what was under them, although he did acknowledge he had made "corrections." Mark also pointed out to Balnick that several dates in his office records were incorrect when compared to other sources. Balnick offered no explanation, just shrugging when the discrepancies were brought to his attention.

> MARK: What prompted the emergency Caesarean, Doctor?
>
> BALNICK: Fetal distress. I noted signs of fetal distress at about 8:00 PM.
>
> MARK: What signs are those?
>
> BALNICK: Irregular fetal heartbeat, meconium staining.
>
> MARK: The record shows heavy meconium staining, not just meconium staining, isn't that correct, Doctor?
>
> BALNICK: Yes, it shows heavy meconium staining, sir.
>
> MARK: Can you explain the significance of the two—meconium staining and irregular heartbeat, Doctor?
>
> BALNICK: Yes, certainly. Meconium staining is usually a sign of fetal distress. It means that the fetus had a bowel movement. It is a greenish substance. The amniotic fluid is stained. The

irregular fetal heartbeat is perhaps a more serious sign the fetus is in distress.

Throughout the afternoon, Balnick had enthusiastically given explanations to medical terms. His enthusiasm always surprised me. Mark let him say whatever he wanted to say. In fact, Mark would speak quietly, almost casually, to Balnick, but always aggressively to White and DeSapio.

Mark continued questioning Balnick about the first time he had been in the hospital. Balnick insisted several times that he had been there at 3:30 PM. Lorraine had been examined frequently until the Caesarean was done at 8:30 PM on March 2.

The examination before trial was finally over shortly before seven.

Mark was more than pleased. The examination reports were full of holes. It was clear to him the examination marked for 3:30 PM was, in fact, done at 3:30 AM. Probably a handwriting expert would be able to clarify it. There were several inconsistencies in the examination reports, too. And why would there be only two examinations during a twenty-four-hour delivery period? The case looked very solid, Mark said. Once he examined the other doctors named in our complaint, we would be well on our way. He would keep in touch with us.

It was clear to me Balnick was lying. I did not know what time he arrived at the hospital, but I knew it was after 3:30 PM, as he had insisted several times during his testimony. I wondered why a supposedly responsible member of the medical profession would not go to the hospital, which was only fifteen minutes away, to examine a patient giving birth to a baby. Not only why he would not go, but also why would he lie when he did not do so?

NINETEEN

The first IUD Lorraine had had put in slipped, and so she went back to have a second one put in. Menstruation was always painful for her, and she experienced greater pain, seemingly with each period, after the second IUD was put in. The pain kept increasing for over a year, and Fanny and I were able to convince her to go to a gynecologist to have a check-up.

She chose Dr. Morgan, another Manhattan physician with a large practice and fees to match. Morgan quickly spotted problems with the two IUDs and Lorraine went into the hospital for a hysterectomy. One of the IUDs had perforated her uterus, and Morgan said the complete hysterectomy was not done a day too soon. She would have to restrict her activities for several months, but, fortunately, there were no signs of malignancy in the lab results.

Meanwhile, Heather had been battling a heavy and persistent cold for several weeks. Her physician, Dr. Roth, suggested hospitalizing her along with Lorraine, so that I'd be able to work and tend to them both. Fortunately, Heather improved, and all I had to do was to arrange for a nurse to take her off the school bus and care for her until I could get home. Lorraine would be in the hospital for ten to twelve days.

While she was in the hospital, Lorraine shared her room with a German woman named Greta, who gleefully informed us that she was terminally ill. In spite of being near the end, Greta complained, she could not get a decent meal, not even a passable cup of coffee. In the meantime, she would greedily consume anything that came into the room. Lorraine did not dare let any of her food lay around because Greta would quickly finish her meal and then move on to Lorraine's tray. I noticed her eating rose petals, and I once saw her chewing a candy bar without removing the paper.

It was clear that Greta was essentially harmless, but I was uncomfortable leaving Lorraine in the same room with her. Her behavior was bizarre, to say the least. After I discussed the situation with Dr. Morgan, he let Lorraine come home two days early.

The trip home from the hospital was excruciating for Lorraine. Every time the car hit a bump, an unavoidable happening on the roads of New York City, she would wince with pain. When we finally got home, Lorraine cried for several minutes when she saw Heather. She had never expected to see "the baby" again, she said.

Though she was in no condition to do it, Lorraine insisted on changing Heather's entire outfit right then. Only she knew how to care for her child, she said. Mothers absolutely knew better than any father what little girls should wear. When I went to answer the telephone, Lorraine left the room, too. Heather was left unattended on our bed, and she immediately rolled onto the floor.

Lorraine started to cry again. I did not love her, she told me. I was letting Heather get hurt to show my hatred of her, "the poor baby's mother." What's more, I always hated her mother and the rest of her family, who were now the only hope she had in the world. The outburst was short. After it was over, Lorraine went to bed to get, she said, some much-needed rest. She had never been able to sleep in the hospital. Heather's outfit remained unchanged.

The next day was a Monday. A nurse was coming to care for Heather from the time she got home from the UCP school at 3:00 PM until I got home from work. I got Heather ready for the program, put her on the bus, and went to work.

Lorraine was awake when I got out of bed, so I explained to her, for the third or fourth time, what the procedure would be. She was asleep again before I had finished feeding Heather breakfast, and did not awaken when I took her out to meet the school bus.

At this time I was working for a large real estate company in Queens. My boss was a man who was held in abject fear by nearly everyone in the company. It took a tremendous amount of courage for my secretary to interrupt a meeting presided over by this man to tell me I'd better talk to Lorraine.

"Why is she calling?" I asked my secretary.

"I can't make it out, but something seems to be terribly wrong."

When I got to the telephone, Lorraine demanded, "Where's the baby?"

"Heather? She went to her program. Where do you think she is?"

"Don't be smart with me, you vicious son-of-a-bitch. She was here last night. I saw her this morning until you left. Where is she now?" Lorraine was nearly screaming into the telephone. I had to hold my earpiece away from my ear, which means that others in the area of my office also got to hear her screaming.

"Honey, she went to school. She's been going to school a while now."

"Oh ... oh ..." Lorraine lowered the volume of her voice. "I remember now. But how can I get her home? You know I can't leave the house. She can't stay in school." When Heather started at the UCP program, Lorraine had to take her there and fetch her home. She used taxis, rides with friends, or whatever means of transportation that was available. Now she sounded as if she were about to start crying again.

"The bus will bring her home. The nurse will take her off the bus. The nurse will come into the house to meet you before the bus comes. Answer the doorbell when you hear it, and let her in. She will take care of Heather until I can get home."

"The nurse?"

"Yes, she—" I started to explain the procedure once more to Lorraine.

"I remember, I remember now. What is her name?"

"Nancy. Nancy Ryan. She will be in uniform and have ID."

"Will she come to the house before she takes Heather off the bus?"

"I don't know. Maybe, but I doubt it."

"Does she have the keys to the house?"

"Yes," I said.

"You mean you gave the keys to my house to some stranger?" Lorraine's voice was getting loud again.

"Yes," I repeated, "because she had to get into the house while I was working, and you were in the hospital. I told her to ring before she comes into the house today."

"Some stranger has the keys to my house?"

I could feel my own anger rising. I have found that anger usually only inflames a situation and, what is more, in my own case, I have trouble letting go of an angry feeling. Once angry, I tend to stay angry for a long time.

Expressions of feelings other than anger have been more successful for me in dealing with difficult people. I have, for a long time, worked very hard to control anger when I feel it. Few people have heard me raise my voice, and fewer still have ever seen me in a rage of any kind.

Lorraine, however, was becoming the focus of a towering rage. It was not enough that I had a fifty- or sixty-hour-a-week job. Or that I did everything in the house, including, at this time, the cooking. Or that I had to care for a helpless daughter. Now Lorraine had decided to go nuts. It was too much. It was also unfair to think this way, I told myself. I recovered a little patience.

"There is no other way we could do it," I said. "Nancy had to let herself in."

"Will she give me back the keys today?"

"If you ask her to, she will. Do you want me to come home now?"

"No, you don't have to. I'm not sure that I could stand to see you, anyway. I need to rest. That's what I am doing—resting."

As I hung up the telephone, Laurel Day, the head of another department for the company, walked into my office uninvited.

"It is," she said, "very surprising to see Ken Zarecor angry."

I gave Laurel a hostile look. For a second, she seemed like a very convenient target for the entire load of anger I was feeling. But she was not part of the problem. I took a deep breath and exhaled slowly.

Laurel sat quietly for a minute or so before I said, "I think Lorraine's hysterectomy went to her head. I get the impression she's going off her rocker." I recounted the conversation I had just ended.

"Kenny," she said, "I've seen many women react strangely to a hysterectomy." She shook her head. "It's too bad, this whole bloody thing. Can I suggest something?" Laurel continued without waiting for an answer from me. "Send her for help. Find a therapy group, a therapist, or something. The very first possible second she is allowed out of the house, she should go for help. Don't let her stew in the house and dwell on herself and her problems."

I thanked her, and said I would think about it. I also said that any decision to seek counseling would have to be Lorraine's. Laurel left my office, but called me about an hour later.

"Yes?" I said as I picked up the telephone.

"Kenny, it's me, Laurel Day. I hope I didn't offend you by sticking my nose in where it's not wanted a while ago."

"Nonsense. I'm planning to send Lorraine to a therapist as soon as she can get out of the house. The advice was good."

"Fine. There is something else I wanted to say. I hope you won't be offended at this, either." Laurel paused as if waiting for some encouragement from me to continue.

"I won't know if I'm offended until I hear it," I said, not really wanting to encourage her.

"Well, I think it would help you if you went for some therapy yourself."

I had to laugh. Laurel laughed with me. "Listen, I don't think you're nuts, or anything like that, it's just ..."

"I know," I said, still laughing. "Whatever your reason, you're probably right."

In a matter of a few days, Lorraine was going to a therapy group at a nearby city hospital and to a weekly private session with a therapist in Manhattan. She could walk to the therapy group, and the therapist sent a car to take her into Manhattan and back.

The therapy group also enrolled Lorraine in a program to polish her office skills. Lorraine enjoyed the classes, but her typing and shorthand skills were already far above the rest of the class, and, in fact, better than those of the instructors. The group was involved in doing volunteer office work for a city hospital. Lorraine did the jobs easily and well, but did not like giving her "high-priced talents" away for nothing.

"I am not a slave," she would say. "These people certainly never did anything for me. Why should I do anything for them?" She felt she was being taken advantage of and the group therapy sessions and volunteer work were dropped in a short time.

The New York real estate business is certainly not for the faint-of-heart, and my job was a difficult one. When I took the job, I found myself among a large group of petty bureaucrats, each and every one of whom jealously and venomously guarded what was deemed to be their "territory." I considered the pettiness as trivial and even sometimes funny, but it was also irritating and tiring. To be fair with this crowd and my employer, however, they seemed to understand, and were tolerant of, the fact that I had fallen far behind in my work. Nobody at the office complained about that, or about the fact that I had to wait to put Heather onto the school bus each morning and was always thirty or forty-five minutes late.

When Lorraine started going to group therapy and the therapist, I hoped that I would be able to stay late at the office to catch up on my work. Lorraine also seemed ready to go to the supermarket and buy two or three things during the week. We could do the bulk of the shopping together on the weekends.

"Oh, no, I can't go by myself," Lorraine told me. "I don't want to. Why can't you do it?"

"I won't be home in time. You can do it. You go to the hospital, so you can go to the store."

"Ohhhh—no, no, no. I can't. Honey, don't make me. Please don't make me. Whenever I go into the street, I see colors. I see big blobs of blues and reds. I need sunglasses. With sunglasses, the colors might go away. Give me sunglasses. Maybe then I can go to the store." Lorraine put her hands to her head and swayed. This was a movement I had seen from her mother on a few occasions when Fanny was agitated or not getting her way.

"You have sunglasses." I took two pair from a drawer and handed them to her. "Go to the store and get the things we need."

This was the beginning of Lorraine's passion for sunglasses. While she always tended to repeat herself—saying three or four times what need not be said at all, and saying things she considered to be important dozens of time—in the next five or six weeks, I was to hear she needed sunglasses hundreds of times.

The day after this conversation, I arrived at the office my usual thirty minutes late. My secretary told me Lorraine had called three times with the same message: "I need sunglasses."

There was no answer when I called her back. During the next month, Lorraine refused to pick up the telephone and would not answer when she was home alone. There was no way of knowing who was on the other end of the telephone when it rang, she told me. Lorraine was certain people were trying to call her to butt into her private business. She would call me, which she did as often as eight or ten times a day, but she would not answer when I, or anyone else, called her.

As the morning progressed, Lorraine called three more times to demand sunglasses. The colors, she said, were getting worse.

A repetition of the fact that she had several pairs of sunglasses would lead Lorraine to change the subject momentarily. "You're always telling me to be neat, but you left your coffee cup on the kitchen table. Why can't you be neat yourself? Why should I be neat when you're always sloppy and inconsiderate?" Or she would complain, "You didn't make the bed this morning. You know Ma is coming over to see me. What will she think when she sees how messy the bed is?"

"You were in the bed, Lorraine, when I left."

"You know Ma wants to see a neat, clean house," Lorraine went on, as if not hearing what I had said.

"So clean it." I told her.

The sunglasses obsession continued several weeks. At its peak, I counted twenty-three messages from Lorraine, which my secretary had taken, in a single workweek. Each message slip had a single word: SUNGLASSES. Lorraine had already given me the same message directly more than a dozen times that week.

Obsessive behavior became a part of our life together. Sometimes the obsessions were funny—such as her addiction to soap operas. Lorraine became so involved with "her stories" that she actually took notes as she watched. I would be regaled in vivid, agonizing detail about the tribulations of her favorite characters.

Other obsessions had some rewards, such as her fascination with cooking. Lorraine purchased dozens of cookbooks, and some nights I would come home from work to find enough food to feed several families prepared. She became a first-rate cook, but in the process cooked literally hundreds of pies, cakes, and whole meals that could not possibly be consumed by our little family.

At other times she became deeply immersed in the politics of the country. She came to detest Richard Nixon, and wrote to him several times a week to make that point. At a later time, she turned her anger toward Bill and Hillary Clinton. When these two were in power in Washington, Lorraine would sit and scream obscenities at them every time they appeared on the television screen. This part of the obsessive behavior was alarming and, on the few occasions that I pointed out to her that screaming vile language at the television was not exactly acceptable behavior, I was subjected to a tirade of verbal abuse against my entire family. In these harangues, she would tell me that I was at fault because she was ill, my family hated her because she was Jewish, and every one of us should "eat shit and die," etc., etc.

Lorraine continued to be afraid to go out alone for several months. She thought people were looking at her and laughing because of her weight and because she had a handicapped daughter. "They" were planning to attack her. When she finally overcame these fears, she did a total turnaround, and it became virtually impossible to keep her in the house during the day. Once she started going out, she would leave the house as soon as Heather was on her bus. She would go out regardless of the weather and she would not return until Heather was due to get home from her program. She would go to the beach, the library, movies, shopping (shopping would become another of her obsessions)—her own house seemed to be the last place she wanted to be.

TWENTY

I followed Laurel's advice and sought counseling myself. My therapist was a man named Pat Barclay. This was not my first experience with therapy. Pat was, in fact, my third therapist, but each of the previous experiences had been limited to three or four sessions each. Therapy seemed to be a dead-end and of no value to me. It was probably useful for someone dealing with immediate and serious issues, but I really did believe therapy was much more than a waste of my time. Nonetheless, I went to see Pat one afternoon before going home.

At our first session, Pat asked me what I thought I would get out of therapy.

"Help," I said.

"Help for what, exactly?"

"Help, I guess, to be able to go on with my life, and to be able to deal with it."

"But you are dealing with it. You take care of your daughter, you support your wife, and you keep a good job. What else do you think you should be doing?"

"I should be able to live my life without—but, wait—I'm not certain I'm alive at all. Weeks pass and I can't remember what happened. I don't remember what I've done, who I've seen, nothing. A lot of the time I start to do things, only to discover that I have already done them—"

Pat was quiet for a few minutes. Then he said, "The most obvious feature about you, as you present yourself, is a huge amount of tension in your body. It's my intuitive feeling that you're trying to stop feeling any pain. You seem to be trying to cope by shutting down, but all you are really achieving is physical tension. You are shutting out all physical sensation. That's the feeling of numbness you have, I would say. We'll see. I would like to work on it with you, but first, let me ask—what do you expect?"

I shrugged. "I'm not sure."

"I think I can help you deal with the problems you face and get on with your life. I try to get my patients to accept that life is a process of living, corny as that sounds. Life is a whole series of events. Some can be good, some bad. But it proceeds, good or bad. People tend to let their problems stop them from breathing—like your breathing is very shallow right now—which, in turn, stops them from experiencing the simple stuff that gives quality to being alive—like tasting food, enjoying company of others, etc."

Pat reached over and began massaging my shoulders, something that he would do often. He believed it was important to touch others, literally touch them, at all times. During my most difficult sessions—and there were many of them—he would always position himself to be able to stroke my hand or massage me.

"Obviously, therapy is not going to make your problems go away," Pat continued, "Just because you'll be able to use your senses more fully, and be more responsive to your environment, your therapy will not make your wife stronger and more independent. It will not mean that your daughter will learn to walk or talk. Therapy will, among other things, show you how you're using your body in reacting to events of your life. It can help you see your actions clearly, in the context of your life, and you will be able to change what you want changed with the help of that new knowledge."

Most of the middle-class people my age I know have been in one kind of therapy or another. Some of my friends have been in therapy for six or even eight years. Of all those I know who have undergone the process, and whose therapy I know something about, I would say no more than two were actually helped by it. I am one of the two.

Early in the therapy, Pat helped me recover from my childhood a startling fact. I did not speak until I was nearly five. According to recollections I recovered in the process of the therapy, I only started talking when Granny told me I had to talk, or otherwise I would not be able to go to school. Starting to speak at five meant I went to school speaking barely intelligible English.

My classmates called me "Dutch" because they were not always certain what language I was speaking.

Not speaking until I was five was not a sign of arrested development. It was a reaction to my environment. There was always competition for attention in my family. So I chose not to compete. To this day, my first reaction in times of stress is to shut up. Lorraine would often complain, "You don't talk! Say something!" Every time she said that, I would quietly and calmly reply, "I would say something, but it's rude to interrupt."

The dream that did much to sustain me during this time was my dream to sing. I had studied singing in London and studied off and on in New York. While I could not surrender the dream, I also did not do the basic groundwork to become a musician. I performed with amateur groups, and did get encouragement from excellent musicians, but doing music professionally was not an option.

At one time, a friend from one of the amateur groups I performed with got me an audition with a small opera house in Germany. Much to my surprise, I was tentatively offered a series of performances as Pinkerton in *Madama Butterfly*. I did some preparation, but did not honestly consider going because it would have meant being in Germany while Heather was in the States. During one of our sessions, Pat asked me how I felt about that. I told him about a kid I knew when I lived in London. He was studying classical languages, but got into some difficulty with his university doing pot or some other low-level drug. To remove him from temptation, his parents more or less forced him to go on a medical (nonreligious) mission to Africa. When he returned to London, he changed his subject to medicine. When I asked him what happened to the study of Classical Greek and Latin, he said that after what he had seen and been through in Africa all that seemed very trivial. In the face of real life, he said, he needed do something that was not so self-indulgent. I have an absolute love of opera and theater, and am very grateful to have been able to see the performances I attended, and I appreciate and value the people who pursue the arts, but, for me, my priority was my little family.

Putting all the pieces of my life—Heather, the lawsuit, Lorraine's problems, limiting my own life and career choices—into one large package, as I was attempting to do, would mean that nothing would ever happen except frustration and growing anger. Deal with one thing at a time, Pat advised.

When I learned again to cry about Heather, I learned to accept that I was not at fault for her retardation. The fact I could not make her walk, talk, or see did not mean I was inadequate or evil. I accepted that I could not live her life for her. Whatever the meaning of this little girl's life, it is not that my life should end because hers will never really begin, and will always be confined to a very narrow range of activities. No purpose could possibly be served by using Heather as a shield to prevent feelings, hope, success, or even failure of goals and dreams. My helplessness in correcting the situation certainly should not prevent me from such everyday pleasures of life as a deep breath, friendships, enjoying food and wine, or watching the ocean roll in and out.

Since Heather's birth, both Lorraine and I had devoted a huge amount of the time and energy available to us trying to deal with her welfare. Our lives were tied up in it. Every action we took or discussed began and ended with how it would affect our ability to care for Heather. For months before her hysterectomy, and for months after it, Lorraine and I did nothing together, unless it involved some facet of Heather's care. As simplistic as it may sound, I suddenly realized one day that Heather's problems were not the entire day. First, Heather laughed, ate, slept soundly, enjoyed the sounds and company of her parents and people at her program, and went on to whatever was next. Heather, in this sense, was smarter than both of us: she was living her life without complaint or recrimination.

Heather's days, in other words, were not given over to what she could not do. Why should ours be? What happened to Heather was a tragedy, but life itself is not tragic. The damage done to my child happened, and the effects of the damage will be with us as long as she lives. So get over it and get on. As Lorraine once said, it is worth one good cry. After the cry, she said, we had to live the rest of our lives. Good advice, excellent advice.

We were not doing that. Both Lorraine and I were frozen in postures of self-pity and helplessness. That realization was painful. But the realization that I should and could do something about it was even more painful.

TWENTY-ONE

After six months in therapy with Pat, I found the strength to face facts about my marriage. Any feelings I ever had for Lorraine were not only dead, they were chopped into a thousand tiny pieces. When I met her, she had been a chubby, bubbly little lady with a mildly irreverent view of the world. Now she seemed to think the world was out to do harm to her and to her child, and I was her chief enemy.

Lorraine no longer laughed; she was no longer cheerful and optimistic. Nothing interested her for long, and she would break into tirades of abuse against me or any interruption to her own plans or attempts to get her to go beyond this little world. She became increasingly heavy, and other physical problems began to appear. In the year after her hysterectomy, she was diagnosed with diabetes. Her personal hygiene, for periods of several months, was nonexistent. Any suggestion that she should change her clothes and clean up would bring a loud, angry outburst and, on a few occasions, a fit of crying.

Fortunately, Lorraine learned to control the verbal abuse five or six months after her operation. The abuse would return now and again, and the obsessive behavior never disappeared. During her political phases, Lorraine would spend hours each day making telephone calls and writing letters to her targets. To my horror, Lorraine told me that she occasionally signed my name to her letters, just so the people being addressed—being berated, actually—would not think some "crackpot" was writing poison-pen letters two or three times a day. (Of course, some "crackpot" was.)

True physical intimacy disappeared after the second IUD was put in. It made sex for Lorraine painful. We both knew that the smart thing to do at that time was to return to the doctor to have the placement corrected, but Lorraine was afraid after two failed attempts. I was also more than a little put off by her heaviness and by the way she stopped taking care of herself physically. The final straw came when Lorraine told me the only important people to her were Heather and her mother. She said she only tolerated me because she needed help with the child. Without a show of anger, but very deliberately, Lorraine told me whatever physical needs I had, I could satisfy elsewhere. She said I should find "it" where I could, but there was no reason to expect she had any desire or "duty" to be my wife "in that way."

One surpassing difficulty with becoming aware is that awareness often indicates the need for change. In some cases, radical change is indicated. I could no longer pretend I had a marriage except in name and responsibility. My only reason for hanging around at all was Heather. It was clear that Lorraine was having serious emotional problems, but it was also clear that she refused to accept my sympathy, let alone any offer of help I might make. I was not at all certain we were doing the right thing for Heather, or for us, by keeping the child at home. There was no acceptable alternative that I could see, but we were not even seeking one.

It was clear our marriage had failed. That realization raised another question: could we, or should we, attempt to save it? I did not consider a marriage counselor for more than a few minutes. Lorraine said she felt all counselors would be against her and would be on my side. She said she had seen the last counselor she needed, or would ever need. Other than the fact that I was subjected to verbal abuse on occasion, the reason Lorraine and I stopped talking to each other were quite simple: we had a basic and seemingly irreconcilable difference about caring for Heather. Lorraine would not discuss the subject further because she was fearful I would take Heather from her. It is here that my basic reticence did not help us: I could not discuss the subject because I have never been one to waste breath if I thought I was not being heard. Even when people are clearly hearing what I am saying, I usually try to say as few words as I possibly can. In answer to my own question, the marriage, as it existed, could not and probably should not be saved. For my own health and mental stability, I should take my leave.

My only concern, once I faced the fact that I should leave, was how Lorraine would be able to cope with Heather. When Heather came home from school, Lorraine did an acceptable job of caring for her. This, to me, was a total contradiction of all that I saw and heard, because Lorraine was usually unclean herself. She seemed to be unfocused and hostile, but Heather was always attended to with love and care. While Lorraine seemed to resent me and, for that matter, nearly all the rest of the world, her attention to Heather was good and gracious. This contradiction baffled me, and made me angry. If Lorraine was capable of fulfilling that job, why did every other aspect of her life suffer? Oddly, once I realized this situation existed, I came to like Lorraine more as a person. Whatever her feelings for and treatment of me, she remained a champion of Heather. There is no doubt in my mind that Lorraine did not consciously make a decision to chase me away, or to protect Heather to the exclusion of virtually everyone, and everything, else in her life. That is what her actions did, however. It may seem callous, but the truth is that I quickly got over any feeling of hurt—I came not to care one way or the other how Lorraine felt about me. What was important to me was the fact that Lorraine was, for her daughter, a good, kind, and protective person.

I spent several months trying to coax Lorraine to go back to school, or to do volunteer work, or do anything that would bring some focus, other than Heather, into her life. She should, I said to her on several occasions, have some life beyond caring for Heather. I gave up when she said, after we talked about her going back to Hunter College and getting her degree, "You aren't trying to get me out of the house so you can send the baby away, are you? I know you want to take her away from me. Ma said you'll keep trying until you do it." What I had feared most—that keeping Heather at home could, in the end, effectively destroy two and probably three lives—seemed to be happening before my eyes.

My final decision to leave took several months to carry out. I kept thinking I would wait until the lawsuit was settled. This quickly turned out to be an unreasonable expectation. By the time I first thought about leaving, the court case was six years old, and was not, as yet, on a court calendar. And the insurance companies for the doctors and the hospital had indicated absolutely no interest in settling our claim out of court.

Another of my personality quirks manifested itself: I had completely mastered the fine art of procrastination. My initial reaction to most stressful situations is to delay confronting them. The fact is that some such situations do resolve themselves, but, honestly, most don't. Lorraine became increasingly intolerable, and procrastination was no longer an option. One Sunday morning I told Lorraine she should sit down at the kitchen table and listen to something I had to tell her.

"Do you want some breakfast?" she asked. "I could make you some eggs."

"No, I don't want breakfast."

"Well, you should eat something. You can't go all day without eating something."

"Stop fussing, Lorraine," I said. "If I get hungry, I'll eat later."

"Okay, but be sure you do." She stood, starting to leave the kitchen. "You don't eat right. It's your own fault. It certainly isn't mine."

"Wait," I said, "I haven't talked to you."

"Oh. Okay. Hurry up, will you? You take forever to get things out sometimes. I am taking the baby over to Ma's."

Lorraine came back to the kitchen table and sat down. She began playing with a condiment carousel in the middle of the table. After she rearranged the salt and pepper shakers and the sugar bowl on it, she lifted the carousel and jumped up to take it somewhere else. Getting her attention had not been easy in the past several months, but keeping her attention was even more difficult. I decided to make my point without any kind of preface: "Lorraine," I said, "I'm moving out of the house one month from today."

She returned to the kitchen table, sat the carousel down, and then picked it up again. Her eyes were wide with disbelief. "You're leaving in one month—you're moving out?"

"That's what I said. I'm leaving one month from today."

Lorraine shook her head and a finger at me. "You're going because you always wanted to. You never wanted really to be married in the first place. You always wanted out. I have done absolutely nothing to deserve you deserting me. You want to leave because of Heather—ever since Heather came—"

"No," I said. "I am not leaving because of Heather. I'll even take her with me, if you want me to. I am leaving because of you."

"No, no. You absolutely will not take my baby. She can't grow up with only her daddy or only her mother. Kids who grow up that way grow up warped and evil. They grow up wrong, and have trouble in later life—" Lorraine was speaking loudly and rapidly. Suddenly she stopped speaking and shrugged. After a short pause she said, "I guess you've decided already.

I knew this was going to happen. That's why I don't care anymore. There's nothing I can do about it."

I remained silent.

"There's nothing I can do about it," she repeated after another short silence. "I'll be left alone here with the baby." Lorraine gave me a long, questioning look, as if she were searching for something to say.

"I'll help you keep Heather home as long as you want to or are able to do it." I was trying to speak very calmly, but I am not certain I was too successful. "I will not stay here with you. There has been no marriage relationship between us for a long time now. Whenever you are upset, you seem to think it is your right to curse, threaten, and otherwise abuse me—" I could feel anger rising in me, so I shut up.

Lorraine sat down, but jumped up from the chair almost immediately. She continued to look at me. As I returned her look, visions of the Lorraine I married came to mind. That Lorraine was not the Lorraine who stood before me now.

She began to cry. As she did, I realized that she had cried very little before her hysterectomy. Before that operation, I had seen her cry once or twice at most. Now almost anything would bring a deluge of tears. After crying for a few minutes, she left the room. "I have a lot to cry about," she said as she left.

A few days later, I got a note from Fanny. She mailed it to me at my office. Fanny asked me to reconsider leaving.

> *Lorraine is a fine, kind woman. I know she has not lived up to your expectations. She has not lived up to mine. Still, she loves you so much. She has loved you from the first day she met you. She told me way back then that "if this boy from Nebraska marries anyone, I hope it will be me." She loves her poor child too much, probably. Can't you overlook her faults and stay, Kenny? God will bless you forever if you do. I will bless you forever if you do.*

Lorraine asked me only once to reconsider. She woke me up one morning at about 1:30 AM to ask. When I said "No," she said she was sorry to have bothered me. She dropped the subject and never again discussed it.

TWENTY-TWO

Before I left, I wrote a letter to the governor of New York State, Hugh Carey. My letter brought to his attention the precious little help we were getting from any agency in the city or state. My letter must have caused some kind of storm between the governor's office and the state agency handling services for retarded children in Brooklyn, because the agency contacted us within days of my mailing the letter to arrange a meeting to discuss our case.

We met with a Miss Lild, a tiny, carefully coiffured lady in a tweed suit and silk blouse, and a Miss Dale, the supervisor of the Brooklyn branch office. Lorraine and I never quite figured it out, but it seemed Miss Lild was from the governor's office, or was the agency's liaison with it. Miss Dale wore blue jeans, a sweatshirt, and hiking boots.

Both ladies were angry with me for writing directly to Governor Carey. If I had a problem, they said, I should have gone directly to the agency. People on staff would be much more willing to offer assistance if they were not "under the gun." Carey was, after all, the governor; the agency—the entire state, it seemed—were dealing with too many problems for the meager resources they had, so I was wasting everybody's time by going directly to him.

"We have been calling," Lorraine interrupted. "And coming here. So far, we've gotten nothing but stalls and excuses. And your current talk seems to want to keep 'em going."

Miss Dale started to respond to that, but Miss Lild interrupted her. "What is it you expect?"

"Help," Lorraine answered. "Only help."

"Help in taking care of Heather," I continued. "Or help in institutionalizing her, if we find that to be necessary at some future date."

"That will not happen as long as I am alive," Lorraine said. "She belongs at home with me."

"There is no longer any such thing as institutionalizing children in New York State," Miss Dale said. "Even if you were to obtain a court order directing institutionalization, the state government probably would not honor it. The governor himself could not order institutions to take a child like Heather. We have not been able to replace the beds taken from Willowbrook and other institutions. We do not have the bed to place her in, and we do not have the staff to adequately care for your daughter."

"What?" I asked. "Do these people run their own little kingdom that is not subject to orders from courts or elected officials?"

"No, it's not like that at all," Miss Lild replied. "It's just that after the Willowbrook consent order, all state institutions will accept only people they can handle."

"Neither the state legislature nor Carey, as you may know from the newspapers, have the political will—guts, actually—to pay for more facilities and workers," Miss Dale added. I could see that Lild was a little uncomfortable with Miss Dale's bluntness, but Dale continued. "You also realize, I hope, that by just adding clients without increasing funding and capacity would only lead to a repeat of the Willowbrook horrors."

After Geraldo Rivera's reports brought the Willowbrook scandal to public attention, the state had agreed, in the Willowbrook consent decree, to reduce the size of the institutional population, improve the care of the resident population, and provide, in Miss Lild's words, "good and adequate" care for patients discharged from the institutions. Many advocates of the handicapped considered this policy of placing small groups of handicapped people in a residential setting to be a major improvement over the old, large institution system, but the program was under strain, due to funding cuts.

"How about the state program of giving financial assistance to send Heather to a 'good and adequate' institution outside New York State?" I asked.

"Not possible," Miss Lild said.

"Absolutely impossible. The funding is simply not available." Miss Dale added.

I pressed the issue. "How does the state government—specifically, how do you ladies, as its representatives—expect parents with a child like Heather to deal with her as she gets larger and older?"

"She could go on a waiting list for one of the residences."

"How does that work?" I asked.

"We just put her name on a list of people needing residential services. When her name comes up, she will be placed," Lild said.

"And that will take how long?"

Miss Dale cleared her throat. "The waiting list is now six or seven years long."

"Suppose there is an emergency situation now?" Lorraine asked.

"We can give you help now, Mrs. Zarecor," Miss Lild said, not answering Lorraine's question. "The state could not, and would not, expect you to bear the burden by yourself."

"I get a little help from Kenny, but it's pretty much what I'm doing now," Lorraine said. "Kenny has to work, you know, and he's involved in other things—"

Both women repeated we could not possibly institutionalize Heather under any conditions at the present time, and future prospects weren't all that bright, either. They believed she would be healthier, happier, and safer at home. I was slightly encouraged to see that Lorraine did at least realize circumstances might force us to do it, but I agreed with her that, in the event of any institutionalization, facilities in New York State should probably be used only as a last, desperate resort. My immediate goal was to try to force this agency to give Lorraine some kind of help.

The conversation of the ladies took on a broken-record aspect: they kept repeating they were "very sympathetic," but unfortunately at this time they could offer nothing but a limited amount of nursing help because of budget constraints.

After Lild and Dale told us about the "help," they brought up the fact that we were now separated. "Well, Mr. Zarecor, leaving will do some good for Heather," Miss Dale said, almost triumphantly. "We do have some good news for you today, Mrs. Zarecor. When he is out of the house, Heather could qualify for Medicaid, and under Medicaid, she could qualify for more nursing help. Plus, you will not have to pay for any medical services or prescriptions she takes."

To start the process of qualifying Heather for more medical services, Lorraine had to go on welfare. In the second month she was on welfare, I was called to family court and told to pay the full amount welfare was paying Lorraine. Lorraine had just started working one day a week with a former employer, again as a medical secretary. Welfare told her she could not work at that job and stay on welfare. She told them, "If my husband is paying the family court every penny you give us, and the family court, in turn, gives that payment to you, how can I be considered to be a welfare recipient?"

Welfare, showing some rare, but welcome, flexibility, agreed. One of their officials called this arrangement "bizarre," and added that they were not meant to be a conduit for support payments. It was arranged that I pay Lorraine the support directly, but both Lorraine and Heather would still be eligible for Medicaid, and, in Heather's case, a Social Security supplement payment.

We had accumulated a large amount of bills before I left. We had accumulated some bills paying for the nursing I hired to help Lorraine and paying for some of the medical experts that examined Heather. None of these costs were huge, but they did add up and always stretched our budget beyond what we could pay from the incomes we had. Also, the economy was in bad shape. Everyone was hurting to some extent. Just a few years previously, we knew many single-earner households; but now nearly every family in our acquaintance had both parents working, and still struggled to make ends meet. We put the costs we could not pay immediately on credit cards.

In my own personal case, my budget was even more stressed. After budgeting for food, rent, and support, I had about ten dollars left to pay off the credit cards and anything else I wanted to do. The solution was maybe too simple: I filed a voluntary bankruptcy, doing all the work myself. The process was painless. There was really nothing to it but filling out the forms, filing them, paying a fee, paying the bankruptcy referee, and going to court for a three-minute hearing. (There have been changes in the bankruptcy law, and I do not know how the process would work currently.)

I saw Heather at least once a week, but there was a time I suffered guilt for "abandoning" her. But "abandoning" is hardly the correct word. When I lived with Heather and Lorraine, we were caught in the classic Great American middle-class squeeze. I made too much money to qualify for any kind of governmental aid except for schooling—Heather's schooling at the

UCP school was paid for by the state and federal governments until she turned twenty-one. Even as that was true, I made far too little to afford many important services for Heather, Lorraine, or myself. There is a sad commentary here. Why should adequate medical care for any person be available only to the rich or the poor? People in all economic classes need medical services and many suffer because of the lack of them. Children with Heather's kind of problems desperately need such services. Why should people in the middle be left to fend for themselves?

Another reason the word "abandoning" is not the right word is simply that Lorraine knew where I was twenty-four hours a day, seven days a week. We talked at least once a day, frequently more than that. No matter where I was, or whom I was with, Lorraine knew how to get in touch with me and frequently did.

Incidentally, Lorraine did not get much nursing help from Medicaid, either. In fact, she ended up with less help than she had when we were paying for it. Medicaid regulations limited nursing aid to specific types of situations (such as a recent hospitalization) that Heather did not qualify for. The twelve hours of nursing assistance initially promised by Misses Lild and Dale never materialized. Medicaid paid for a total of six hours a week. In the end, Lorraine gave up trying to get more. The application process was demeaning and demanding, and the help sent through the program was uniformly inadequate and unreliable.

Just as nobody should think I left to qualify Heather for more and better medical care, nobody should think I left to force Lorraine to accept responsibility for Heather's daily care. Both of these things happened, however. Lorraine was an excellent mother, and she gave Heather much more than just good care. At the time of my departure, I totally disagreed with Lorraine about the prospect of keeping Heather at home indefinitely, but I respected Lorraine for the fact that the one thing she knew was that she should and could provide excellent care for her child.

I left to preserve my own sanity, and I did that.

TWENTY-THREE

Some of Heather's self-abusive behavior was alleviated by the training given to her at the United Cerebral Palsy program. She stopped biting her hand, but she would still suck her thumb unless she had some kind of pacifier in her mouth. We tried the standard baby pacifier, but Heather rejected that and would settle for plastic keys only. The staff at United Cerebral Palsy complained that this was dangerous—she could bite off part of the plastic and choke. I agreed with them, as did all of Heather's doctors, but Lorraine argued that this seemed to be one of the very few pleasures Heather had, so she should not be deprived of it. Heather did eventually learn to sit for long periods without the keys, but when she got home, Lorraine would put the keys back in her mouth.

Unfortunately, shortly after starting the program, Heather started having seizures. The first seizure came on a Friday night. My time with Heather was Friday night to Saturday night. This night as I came into the door, Lorraine was holding Heather in her arms and frantically dialing the telephone. "Oh! Thank God you're here, Ken. The baby is having some trouble. She can't breathe."

Heather had turned a dark reddish color, reminiscent of her color when she was first admitted to University Hospital shortly after her birth. Breathing seemed to be causing her pain. She would inhale slightly and exhale in a gasp.

"Have you called for help?" I asked.

"The police emergency answered. They said an ambulance would be here in ten or fifteen minutes, but that was nearly half an hour ago."

"We can't wait any longer," I said. "We'd better take her to the city hospital ourselves."

There was a city hospital about seven blocks from us. I took Heather from Lorraine, strapped her into her wheelchair, and raced down the street to the hospital.

On the way, Heather lost consciousness. While she was unconscious, the inhalations became easier, but the exhalations still came out in a wheezing sound. Heather recovered consciousness after a few minutes, and the struggle for breath resumed.

At the hospital, an attendant told me to sit down and wait our turn. We would be called, she said, when a doctor could get to us.

Before I could explain why we could not wait, Lorraine said, "No, we won't." She had trailed us as we ran to the hospital, but caught up when we entered the emergency room. "This baby can't breathe. We must see a doctor immediately."

We were taken into the emergency room without waiting. Heather was given a tranquilizer and her breathing became easier.

Heather stayed in the hospital five days. She had suffered an epileptic seizure. The doctor told us that we could expect more seizures. With medication, they could be contained, but not prevented.

Heather did have more seizures, but they were infrequent and less severe until, a year after the first seizure, I got a call at my job from the social worker at the UCP school. "Mr. Zarecor," she said, "Heather has had a series of twelve or fourteen seizures. The staff nurse has advised us to take her to a hospital. I can't reach your wife on the telephone. Can you come? A parent has to approve to take her to the hospital."

"Of course," I said. I gave instructions to the staff nurse to have Heather taken to College Hospital in Brooklyn. I thought we could get a better evaluation and better treatment there than at the city hospital in their neighborhood.

Before I left the office, I called Fanny to see if Lorraine was with her. Fanny did not know where Lorraine was, but I told her to have Lorraine contact the hospital if she should call.

When I arrived at the emergency room of College Hospital, Heather was lying unconscious on the examination table, being fed a clear liquid intravenously.

"You're the father?" a large female doctor with a Russian accent asked as I walked up and took Heather's hand.

"Yes, I am," I said.

"I really didn't have to ask," the doctor said. "You look exactly like her. Where is the mother?"

"I don't know for sure," I said. "Maybe she went to Manhattan. I couldn't reach her."

"You should find her and get her here. This child is about at her end."

All of this sounded familiar. Heather was clearly not in good shape, but this doctor did not know her facility for survival. If it were her time to go, I thought, Heather would be released to, as Socrates said, "a better place." Somehow, however, I doubted this was Heather's time. None of the doctors that hovered around the emergency room knew this kid, except from a cursory examination of the records from UCP that had accompanied her to the hospital.

Lorraine had just gotten home to meet Heather's school bus when I was finally able to reach her. When I told her the doctor said she should get to the hospital as quickly as possible, she sounded calm and said she would be there. By the time she arrived, Heather had been transferred to a room.

"What have they been doing to the child?" she demanded as she came into the hospital room. Her wild-eyed, agitated movements belied her calm manner on the telephone. Her angry looks were directed at me and the medical staff attending Heather.

"They gave her some phenobarbital intravenously," I said.

"No, no," Lorraine said, waving her right hand up and down. "I mean at the school. What did they do there to cause this seizure? I know they stimulate the child too much. We'll have to talk to them about it. Maybe we'll have to take her out of that school, if she continues having seizures."

"The seizures are caused by her physical problems," I told her. "I'm sure nothing at the school causes them."

"How do you know that?" Lorraine was becoming very loud as she spoke. "She never had serious seizures until she started at that school. Why did you send her to that school?"

"Because you said it was time she was in school. Because you said we should move to Brooklyn to get her into a good program."

"It's always my fault, isn't it? You always find some way to blame me, don't you? I want you to know—"

The Russian doctor interrupted Lorraine. "Are you all right? Can I get you something to help you relax?"

"No, Doctor, thank you. It isn't necessary," Lorraine said. "I'll be okay." Indicating me, she added, "But him—he isn't helping."

"Your husband seems like a caring father to me," the doctor told Lorraine, and added, "You really should calm yourself, missus. Even if he were causing problems—and I know he isn't—you need to focus on the child and not surrender to any anger or fear."

Lorraine waved me off. "What is the problem?" She spoke to the doctor but continued to give me hostile looks.

"According to the school, your daughter had a series of gradually more serious seizures, until she lost consciousness," The doctor said. "The seizures are a very serious matter, but are no reason for anger at your husband. And your anger is doing you no good either—"

"I know, I know. I am sorry," Lorraine said. "He just gets on my nerves. How long will Heather be in the hospital?"

"You just walked into the room, and he is already on your nerves? Sensitive nerves—you better do something about them," The doctor said. By this time, I was hoping these ladies would both shut up and get onto the important subject at hand. "She will be here until we can run some tests to see if we can find the cause."

"It's the school that's the cause," Lorraine said. "They stimulate her too much, and Kenny just lets them."

"You said you were going to get off that, Lorraine," I said. "Doctor, how many days or hours will that take?"

"She'll have to recover from this seizure before we can start," the doctor told us.

This was not the first—and certainly not the last—time Lorraine would act irrationally toward me when Heather was in some kind of distress. She would always apologize later. Her apologies never felt sincere to me, and they did not make me feel any better, but I would always accept them.

Heather was in the hospital for over a week before she was allowed to go home. Although the doctors suggested that Heather stay home from the program for at least a week, she was back in it on the first school day she was home. Lorraine said she had missed too much school already and needed to get back to it.

TWENTY-FOUR

In July 1975, Mark Billings called us to a meeting in the offices of Dugan, Tuscano & Billings. He had finally been able to get EBTs from all the doctors listed in our lawsuit. It was clear to him, he said, that we should discontinue action against everyone except Balnick and the hospital, once the trial started. In exchange for discontinuing the action against him, one of the doctors might testify to the fact that the 3:30 PM examination Balnick had signed and claimed as his own in testimony was done without Balnick being in the hospital. A handwriting expert would verify the signature was Balnick's, made over another signature. Mark had copies of the hospital time records proving this doctor was on duty at 3:30 PM. Mark was still not certain what the entries were that Balnick had crossed out, but more analysis of the original record would almost certainly reveal that.

"When will we be going to trial?" Lorraine asked.

"It's hard to say. The court calendars are very crowded," Mark said, "but I think I can apply for special consideration due to the fact that Heather has been hospitalized with major seizures twice in the past year. The trial might be sixteen or eighteen months away, but we're definitely on the last mile. We just have a few little problems with the record to clear up, and we are ready to go."

Mark introduced us to Bill Dugan, who would be trying the case for us. Bill is one of those Irishmen who, as Lorraine put it, could charm birds out of the trees. He also knows it, and uses his talents well. Still, at the first meeting, he seemed a little remote, saying simply that he hoped to be working with us soon.

Before we left the meeting, Mark received a call from the law firm representing the hospital. They were calling to suggest that a settlement could be worked out, but Balnick's insurance carrier would have to agree to pay the majority of any settlement.

"I agree with that," Mark said into the telephone. "But you both should know we are not going to consider any offer under one million dollars."

We could hear the party on the other end of the telephone laughing. We could also hear the voice ask Mark if his clients just happened to be in the office.

"You go to Balnick's carrier and discuss it with them," Mark said. "I would appreciate your getting back to me one way or the other."

After a few more exchanges, Mark hung up.

"They will not, of course, come up with a million dollars," he said. "They might come up with $750,000 though. As a matter of fact, however, while you're here, we should discuss what bottom-line figure you would take to settle this case. Have you even considered it?"

We had not.

"Let me ask you," I said, "since you are the attorney here, what do you recommend?"

"I think that this case is worth, say, $600,000 or $750,000 tops. If we take it to court, we could not get more than that, I would think, after the Appellate Division cuts it down."

"What's that?" I asked. "Do you mean that we could get a judgment of a million dollars, but collect only half or two-thirds of that amount?"

"Yes. The way it works in New York State is that the Appellate Division of the State Supreme Court reviews all judgments automatically. They virtually always reduce the amounts."

"That's unbelievable."

"Unfortunately, it happens every day of the week. Anyway, let me ask you this. Suppose they offered half a million. Would you take it?"

"No," I said, immediately. Realizing that Lorraine had not had a say in the matter, I shrugged. "At least I say no. Maybe we should think about it. Shall we think about it and get back to Mark, Lorraine?"

"Nope, not really," Lorraine said. "I agree with you. After Mark and Mr. Dugan take their cut, half a million won't cover what we'll have to do for the baby. You're right. If they offer anything under, say, $650,000, I vote we turn it down."

"I would vote 'no,' too." I said. "We would consider $650,000, but nothing lower."

"That might be tough," Mark said. "But so far we've been offered nothing. If we should be, I'll keep these instructions in mind."

"Just a minute, Mark," Lorraine said. Speaking to me, she said, "Does Mark have a vote in this matter?"

Mark answered for me. "No, I don't, really. I can advise, but the final decision is yours."

We talked to Mark at infrequent intervals over the next two years. In July 1977, I called him again.

"Mark," I said, "two years ago you said the case was on the last mile, and we would come to trial in sixteen or eighteen months. What's the delay? When can we expect to go to trial?"

"I don't remember saying that, Ken. If I did, I'm sorry. I did not mean to get your hopes up. But we're really not in a position to make that kind of promise. The court calendars are so overcrowded, it often takes five or six years for a case to get to the trial phase."

"In a few months, Mark," I said, "this case will be seven years old. Can you give me any idea when it might go to trial?"

"I'm sorry, but I really cannot commit us. There are just too many intangibles involved. Court calendars … when doctors are available to testify … when attorneys are available to try the case, when a courtroom is available, and so on. I really couldn't say."

I hung up from talking to Mark and immediately dialed another number—the number of another famous malpractice law firm in Manhattan—Glass & Berns. I said I wanted to talk to them about taking a case from Dugan, Tuscano & Billings, and to let them prosecute it. Mr. Berns Jr. said that I should come to talk to him that very afternoon.

Mr. Berns Jr. could not have been two degrees warmer than death itself. If he's this old, I thought, how old must Mr. Berns Sr. be? Nevertheless, Mr. Berns Jr. listened carefully to my story about our case. Mr. Berns seemed to know about the case. I wondered if he had already talked to Mark or Bill Dugan about it.

"Why do you want to take it away from Mark's firm?" he asked after I finished my narration.

"Frustration," I said. "It's been seven years. We—"

"What you're doing is not all that unusual, really," Mr. Berns said. "In fact, just last week I won a case the client had threatened to take away on two separate occasions. Now he's very grateful he did not leave us.

"Let me tell you about this case, as I see it," Berns continued, leaning back in his large chair and lighting up the foulest-smelling cigar I have ever encountered. "You should get a big recovery out of it. It's sad, but vital, I guess. Sad, because it won't restore your daughter in any way, but vital for the safekeeping of her and your own health and well-being. You have a right to expect some kind of reasonable and expeditious handling of your case. Justice delayed is, as every two-bit law professor in the world says dozens of times each semester, justice denied. Still, you should think carefully about what you're doing."

Without waiting for me to respond, he pushed a letter in front of me. It was addressed to Mark Billings. The letter asked the firm of Dugan, Tuscano & Billings to turn all files on the case over to the firm of Glass & Berns. "Sign there, please. We'll get the files and start working on them next week."

I signed the forms and called Lorraine to tell her what I'd done. The matter was closed, I said, but I should call Mark to tell him why I had changed law firms. Mark was gone for the weekend, his secretary said. He always leaves about 2:30 PM on Fridays during the summer.

At this time I was living in a small apartment in Queens. After my appointment with Berns, I went back there to get ready to go to Brooklyn and spend Friday night and Saturday with Heather.

The telephone was ringing when I walked in my front door. It was Ron Tuscano, of the firm of Dugan, Tuscano & Billings. Had I signed the case over to Glass & Berns? If I was having difficulty with Mark, why hadn't I contacted him? Could he ask me what the problem was?

I was surprised and not in the least amused. His law firm had not shown so much interest in the seven years they had the case. I did not say that, but I did say it appeared to me that after seven years with them, the case had gone nowhere. It was time to let somebody else take it. Lorraine and I could not wait forever to see if they could handle it. The matter was, as far as I was concerned, closed.

When I got to Brooklyn, Lorraine looked upset.

"What's the matter?" I asked her. "I bet I can guess."

Lorraine laughed. "Did Bill Dugan call you?"

"Dugan? No, Ron Tuscano called me. Dugan called you?"

"Yeah, he did. What did you tell Tuscano?"

"I said the matter was closed. What did you tell Dugan?"

"I told him he'd have to talk to you. Are you sure we want to do this?"

"I don't see that we have a choice," I said. "They had this thing for almost seven years. And so far, we seem to be nowhere. Now I think we should move on and try to get it settled one way or the other."

Lorraine shook her head, "Are you going to tell that to Mr. Dugan?"

"Yes, I will, if he calls me. I told it to Tuscano, so why shouldn't I tell it to Dugan?"

"No, reason, I guess," Lorraine said, "But Bill seems more like a *mensch* than either Mark or Tuscano. He also said Mark had laid a strong foundation to try the case. It doesn't seem fair to take the case away now—"

"There is no such thing as fairness in this world," I said. "If there were any fairness in the world, Nixon would die in jail and Heather would be walking. It's time we got someone who can settle the case, period."

"Bill said he would call you. Are you going to talk to him?" Lorraine asked.

"If he calls, I will talk to him. I, personally, don't think he'll call me."

That Sunday night, I was staying over at a friend's when Lorraine called.

"Mark called me a while ago, Kenny," Lorraine said. "He wants to talk to you. Please talk to him. He cried. He actually cried."

"I'll call him tomorrow. Monday morning."

"Oh, come on, honey. Don't make him suffer. Call him and tell him you'll talk it over with him in the office."

"If you want to discuss it, you can come with me to his office and we'll discuss it. And you can call him and tell him that."

"It won't make him feel better, he knows you are the one who'll decide … I told him, and he knew it anyway. All I said was it was up to you. So please call him. I felt so bad for him when he cried."

I did as Lorraine asked. Mark and I agreed to meet in his office the next day. During the meeting, Ron Tuscano came into Mark's office and said I should let him know if Mark was not doing what I expected. He would serve as a referee between us. Bill Dugan also came in to say it was a good case, Mark had been doing excellent work on it, and he looked forward to trying it.

Mark told me he could understand our impatience, and he would again apply for special consideration from the court. This statement actually annoyed me a great deal. There was no "again" involved: no application for special consideration had ever been made.

Still, I let the matter slide, and Mark continued. "I think the application could say two things: one, the situation is critical because Heather has been seriously ill with seizures; and two, Lorraine desperately needs help in handling the child."

"Can you give us any guess as to when the trial might happen?"

Mark paused for a long minute, and then said, "With or without the granting of my special consideration application, I couldn't say. I don't want to say—I'm in deep enough without digging myself in deeper."

Two weeks later, Mark called me and, after some pauses and throat clearing, told me that, after consultation with Tuscano and Dugan, he was not going to make the special consideration application on the grounds of Heather's health. An issue at the trial would almost certainly be her life expectancy. We should not give the defendants such an easy issue. He would make the application on the grounds that Lorraine desperately needs help.

In the past few years, doctors had been telling us that Heather's life expectancy was greater than that originally predicted for her. Dr. Roth, ever proud of the fact he never hedged his comments or diagnosis (that is a neutral way of saying he seemed to be incapable of graciousness or simple grace when discussing Heather's long-term prospects), told us that Heather might easily live into her thirties or forties and added, "This is, of course, the double-edged sword of modern medicine: people can survive and be kept alive for years even if their lives have no quality or regardless of the burden their care causes the families."

Both of us realized that if Heather survived to be forty, Lorraine would, in turn, be in her late seventies. Predictions of a longer life expectancy for Heather, did not, in truth, make us calmer and more relaxed. An omnipresent issue every parent of handicapped children must face is what will happen to surviving children when the parent can no longer care for them, through infirmity or death. Every facility we knew about that cared for children with

Heather's degree of retardation was not decent, let alone adequate. The lawsuit became more and more important to us. We were more determined than ever to press our case, and although I had respect for the firm of Dugan, Tuscano & Billings, I was beginning to doubt their commitment to it.

As an added annoyance, an application for special consideration was never filed. Mark never mentioned it again, in any case. During the next year, we discussed what was happening on infrequent occasions. The crowded court calendar and the difficulty of assembling all the required parties were the main culprits in not going to trial, according to Mark.

In March 1979, a man identifying himself as Steve Cohn called. He was working on our case in place of Mark Billings.

"What happened to Mark Billings?" I asked.

"He has chosen to disassociate himself from the firm," Steve said.

"That's interesting," I said. "I suppose what it means in our case is that he won't have anything to do with it from now on?"

Steve said nothing further about Mark, but instead told me there was a good chance we'd be able to go to trial in the current term of the State Supreme Court. He would have to talk to both of us. Before that, however, I should go to the State Supreme Courthouse in downtown Brooklyn and meet Ron Tuscano. Ron was going to appear before the calendar judge to press for an immediate trial. It would help his application, they thought, if I showed up, too.

It turned out that there was no court available, and the attorney who would be representing Balnick was not available before June.

"We have a good chance of getting a court and the trial in June," Ron told me.

June came and went. There could be no trial until the fall term. Trials in the early summer are not a good idea in any case, Ron and Steve both assured me, and so this delay was probably a good thing. The heat tends to make people irritable and it is difficult to maintain their concentration.

Summer trial or no summer trial, Lorraine and I had had enough of waiting. I told her I was going to go back to Glass & Berns. Ron told me we could, technically, change attorneys one minute before the trial began. By changing attorneys, we would not lose our place on the court calendar.

As I have said before, I have learned to control my temper, and I probably will not scream or throw things when I do get angry. I might, however, write a poison-pen letter. The letter I wrote to Dugan and Tuscano said they had had the case nearly ten years (I was wrong. They had it nearly nine years when I wrote). That was simply and unquestionably too long. Mark Billings had said we were on the last mile in 1975. That mile had taken four years so far, and we were still running, but getting nowhere. Therefore, I was planning to contact Glass & Berns again, in the hope they could get the case to trial.

When I called to make an appointment with Glass & Berns, Mr. Berns told me that he knew our case was on the court calendar and was sure to be called within the next month or six weeks. He suggested I stay with Dugan and company because they would represent us extremely well. I thanked him for his graciousness and waited to hear from Steve again.

In October, a jury was selected. The jury selection took three days, and then they sat waiting for two weeks until a judge and courtroom became available. We were threatened with a judge who had a long history of personal differences with and animosity toward Bill Dugan. Bill had once told this particular judge he thought the judge was a disgrace to the bench and to the legal profession. Such relationships, clearly, are not conducive to good and fair trials. To compound the problem, this judge, according to several attorneys who had tried cases before him in the recent past, reported he did not hear well. Some said he did not hear well, others said he was stone deaf. If we had to go before that judge, Bill said, he would go on record immediately with a motion that the judge disqualify himself.

We lucked out and got Judge Thomas James as our trial judge. The trial started November 6, 1979, just a few days before the ninth anniversary of my first conversation with Paul Tedesco.

TWENTY-FIVE

When Lorraine and I entered Judge James's courtroom to hear the opening statements, none of the attorneys had arrived yet, but Judge James was sitting at his bench, reading *The New York Times*. He was in the room by himself. He believed that entrances by judges, with everyone standing and awaiting the judge's pleasure, were artificial and unnecessary. He also never wore judicial robes.

Malpractice juries in New York State have six members. Their verdicts do not have to be unanimous, but five jurors must agree to any finding. Our original jury panel consisted of three men and three women, with three male alternates.

"The plaintiff must make a case," Judge James told the jury after the attorneys were in place and the jury sworn in. "Defendants are not required to respond. The evidence and any conclusions concerning this case must be based on medical art and knowledge, as they existed in 1969. Advances in medicine made after 1969 cannot be used by the plaintiff or defense in this case."

The jurors looked expectantly at the judge and nodded, as if in agreement.

"Many counterclaims will be made," Judge James continued. "It will be up to you, the jury, to sort them out; to tell what was true, what was false."

I had confidence the jury would be able to do that, even though they would soon see this was an extremely complex case.

"Now, please give your attention to Mr. William Dugan, who is the attorney for the plaintiffs in this case," the judge said. "He will tell you in his own way how he intends to prove the cause of action for the plaintiffs."

Bill rose and stood before the jury. He was clearly in a good mood and was pleased to be where he was. His good mood, and the friendliness he tried to convey to the jury, would not hold very long.

"An opening statement is a guide for you to follow as the evidence comes in," Bill said. "As I tell you what we are going to say here, you are going to say, 'Well, you better prove it.' We are going to prove it, take my word for it.

"This couple, the Zarecors," Bill said, pointing us out to the jury, "had just been married and were having their first child in 1969. In 1969 Lorraine Zarecor was thirty-seven years old. She was no kid, in the sense of having a first baby. Having a first baby at thirty-seven is a little different, the doctors will tell you, than having a first baby at twenty-one or eighteen. Doctors will testify that Lorraine was an 'elderly prima gravida,' which basically means a woman over thirty-five having a first pregnancy. Nevertheless, the pregnancy was uneventful. We are making no claim about the pregnancy."

The jury was told about the EBTs—the defendants knew what we would say before because of these examinations before trial. We knew what they would say for the same reason. "Well," Bill said, "we might have a few surprises.

"We will make many claims in presenting our case," Bill told the jury. "The first will be our claim that Lorraine had been in labor when she went into the hospital. Dr. Balnick will say 'no.' He said 'no' at the EBTs back in 1975. But Balnick was not there during the night to see his patient. He admitted as much at the EBT. Still, he will claim Lorraine had not been in labor. He will claim the hospital had given him this information."

Bill paused a moment to look around the room for Balnick.

"Then Lorraine was taken to the X-ray room. Balnick admits X-rays were taken. Do we know what is in the X-rays? Do we know what is in the X-ray report? No. Why? They are gone. But more than the X-rays are missing. We charge there was not only negligence in this case, but there was a very crude attempt at a cover-up, and we are going to prove it. Hold me to it."

Bill paused again, letting this statement sink in, and looking, in turn, at us, the jury, and the other attorneys in the room.

"X-rays are done after a woman is in labor for twelve or so hours, to determine if the baby will be born spontaneously. Lorraine was in labor, but ineffectual labor, and the X-rays were taken to determine what should be done next. What the X-ray showed, and we will prove, was a cephalopelvic disproportion. The missing X-rays were taken to determine if the pelvis was a sufficient size to allow the baby to be born."

Bill took a sip of water, consulted his notes, and continued. "Ken Zarecor will testify about a number of calls he made to Dr. Balnick and the hospital. Balnick will not dispute any of Ken's statements. We will show that the doctor still had not seen his patient at noon, or fifteen hours after she had gone into labor. Balnick will claim he arrived at 3:30 PM. We will prove he was not there. In fact, we will prove he was not there until around 7:00 PM, twenty-four hours after Lorraine went into labor. And when he finally did arrive, he found meconium staining. He found an irregular fetal heartbeat. He panicked."

I looked over at the jurors. Several of them, especially the female jurors, were leaning forward.

"Meconium staining is a cardinal sign of fetal distress," Bill explained. "So an emergency Caesarian was done. But it is our claim the damage had already been done. The baby was finally delivered by Caesarian section at about 8:20 PM, seriously brain-damaged. It was too late because of the neglect. That's our claim against Dr. Balnick.

"Our claim against the hospital is on the grounds that they sat back and watched a woman in ineffectual labor for all those hours and did nothing when Balnick did not show up. They may have, furthermore, given Balnick information that was wrong. Balnick had said at the EBT—and I quote—'I was told she wasn't doing anything.'"

Bill sat down. I thought his presentation was excellent. He had started calmly, stating clearly the cause of our legal action. He had built on a statement of the facts, as we would present them, to an emotional close. The jury, who appeared to be equally impressed with Bill's opening, could see we had a solid case and serious charges we could prove.

Judge James introduced the jury to James O'Neill next. He represented the hospital. After acknowledging the court and other attorneys, O'Neill started his response.

"How do you respond to such an opening statement as you have just heard?" he asked. Then, answering his own question, he continued. "Well, we do that by telling you in cold fact what we intend to prove. We will prove Lorraine Zarecor had contractions that were from five to ten minutes apart when she arrived at the hospital. Since Lorraine was in her first labor and pregnancy, the hospital staff could and did expect stronger contractions to indicate the imminent birth of the child.

"We will contend that what the hospital did through its employees was well within the standard of care administered by hospitals in this area in 1969, or even today. They did everything proper for and with Mrs. Zarecor, and they did everything proper with respect to the baby, Heather Zarecor. We say that what happened to Heather Zarecor was not caused or made worse by any action of the staff or the hospital."

O'Neill then sat down. Not bad, I thought. Conservative, but solid. But then the attorney representing Balnick, John Tenuto, got up to finish the opening statements. When he opened his mouth, he immediately changed the course of the trial.

"I think it behooves me," he said, "to say to you that a certain number of areas Mr. Dugan feels are going to be disputed, I don't believe are going to be disputed."

Lorraine and I leaned forward to hear Tenuto better. Bill and Steve sat bolt upright. We all had a feeling he was about to drop a bombshell. And he did.

"Dr. Balnick testified in an examination before trial incorrectly on a number of points. Dr. Balnick will now testify we cannot prove he was in the hospital until around seven o'clock."

Balnick was going to come into court and admit he was not in the hospital until seven at night—twenty-four hours after Lorraine went into labor! I could not believe my ears.

"An unquestioned dispute would be," Tenuto was saying to the jury, "how long is Heather Zarecor going to live?" He turned and looked directly at the two of us as he continued. "This is not an easy case. But Heather's life expectancy will be an item of dispute.

"The jury will be within their rights to find fault with Balnick if his failure to appear is a factor or cause of Heather's present condition." Tenuto went on. "Dr. Balnick had a perfect right to rely upon the information given to him by the hospital."

Tenuto was not through with his surprises. "Dr. Balnick's office records will be shown to be wrong in some instances," he said. But he shrugged off that little fact. "That is neither here nor there. What is important is what other evidence will show.

"The simple truth is it will not be easy for Dr. Balnick to remember much about what happened in this case ten years ago, even though the results were horrendous and astoundingly poor. Errors in the records were made and had to be corrected. And, Dr. Balnick, frankly, did correct those errors. That is the 'cover-up' Mr. Dugan talked about.

"Dr. Balnick will testify he could not possibly have told Mr. Zarecor about the X-ray in the call just before the Caesarian. Those statements made by Mr. Zarecor are 'self-serving.'

"So we have three disputes that you, the jury, will have to decide: one, was there a 'cephalopelvic disproportion,' or some other reason the baby got into such trouble? two, whether the procedure should have been done earlier than it was; and three, should you feel somebody is to blame, the probable longevity of the child.

"Doctors are not gods," Tenuto said, in closing his first statement to the jury. "Despite even the best medical attention, which this mother and child were getting in that hospital, this child was still born in brain-damaged condition, which we say is undoubtedly going to cause considerable shortening of her life, without fault on the part of the hospital or the doctors."

The opening statements were over. Bill and Steve immediately began scrambling to gather material on Balnick. Tenuto's opening statement meant their trial strategy would be dramatically altered. The trial would be much shorter. Balnick would now be the first witness called by us, but before he could testify, Bill would read to the jury parts of his 1975 EBT testimony.

Bill informed the court of his plans for the next day of the trial. Tenuto asked for a sidebar. The attorneys often gathered round Judge James's desk during the trial. I often wondered why they did that: every single word they uttered could be heard plainly throughout the courtroom, including arguments on what testimony would be allowed. At this sidebar, Tenuto said he was not certain if his client would be available to testify the next day or not. Bill said simply that Balnick had been subpoenaed and had no choice. Judge James reinforced that comment, and reminded Tenuto that there would be serious consequences if Balnick did not appear.

At the end of the day, we had, it seemed to me, taken a large step in winning the case. Balnick, or Tenuto, knew the doctor would be caught lying if they tried to stick to the EBT testimony. So Balnick would refute all that testimony and would not try the same lies under Bill's questioning.

Bill told me before the trial that he thought the defendants would listen to three or four days of our evidence and then ask for a settlement. Now I could see this might happen.

Never in the nine long, frustrating years we waited for the trial, did I doubt we could prove our case against Balnick and the hospital. They would be held liable for the negligence. As I went home after the opening statements, I was more certain than ever we would win.

TWENTY-SIX

Lorraine and I were surprised to see the bearded man in a gray suit and leather coat seated in the front row of the public section as we entered the courtroom the following day. Beside him sat a much younger woman.

"Look," I said to Lorraine, "there's Balnick. I wonder who the girl is."

"Is that Balnick?" Loraine asked. "Jeez, I guess it is. That beard really changes him."

We went out of our way to avoid Balnick and the woman. As we sat down, however, he moved closer, until he was sitting directly in front of us.

"Hello," he said.

Neither of us took his offered hand.

"Is that you, Lorraine?"

Lorraine clenched her jaw and grabbed the back of the bench in front of us, as if for support. She quickly removed the hand, however, when Balnick patted it.

"Yes, Dr. Balnick, it is," she managed to get out.

"Good. And how are you, Mr. Zarecor?"

"I am well, Doctor," I said.

"I don't suppose I should be here," Balnick said quietly, starting to move away. But then he stopped, and turned back to look at Lorraine. "I want you to know I hope you get every penny you need to take care of the girl."

He moved back to the young woman.

"What did he say?" I whispered to Lorraine.

Balnick speaks clearly and I hear very well. I just did not believe what I had heard.

"He said he hoped we get every penny we need to take care of Heather," Lorraine said.

"This whole thing gets more incredible with every passing minute," I said.

"You're telling me," Lorraine agreed. "Should we do anything about what he said?"

"I'll tell Steve and Bill, but I don't think there's anything we can do about it, or that it will do us any good." Still, I wrote a note and gave it to Steve. At the first break, they took us into the hall and asked us to repeat the story.

"I don't know what it means," Bill said. "I suspect Balnick desperately wants out. He doesn't want the humiliation of a public trial, but Tenuto won't just let him surrender. This is clearly a case of the attorney representing the interests of the insurance carrier first and the doctor second. The doctor should be the party represented first. We might be able to use this information to force a settlement, however. We'll see."

The morning session opened with Bill reading from the 1975 examination before trial. He read to the jury all the items Tenuto said Balnick would now contradict.

When Balnick was finally called to the witness stand and sworn in, the hospital records were introduced into evidence as plaintiff's exhibit number one. Bill's tone was neither warm nor friendly as he started to question Balnick.

> BILL: Doctor, let me ask you a few questions about your background. Might I ask you first, what is your age, sir?
>
> BALNICK: Fifty-two, today.
>
> BILL: Today? Happy Birthday!
>
> BALNICK: Thanks a lot.
>
> BILL: Well, we're not going to sing "Happy Birthday" for you, but anyway, let's go on. Would you please explain "cephalopelvic disproportion" for the jury?
>
> BALNICK: You can open a door completely and go through easily. If you close the door, no man could go through, but maybe a mouse could.
>
> BILL: In other words, it has to do with the size of the baby and

the size of the opening, to determine whether the baby is going to be born through the opening. Is it one size compared to the other?

BALNICK: No, you are incorrect, sir. (Balnick smiled apologetically.)

BILL (glaring at Balnick): I am incorrect?

BALNICK: You say "only the size of the passenger and the size of the opening." There are other elements to consider—uterine contractions, the condition of the cervix, dilation of the cervix, and so on.

BILL: Would a doctor order an X-ray if a woman had been in labor for twelve hours, but it was an ineffectual labor?

BALNICK: I agree that a doctor would order an X-ray.

BILL: Doctor, did you order an X-ray at seven in the morning for Mrs. Zarecor?

BALNICK: Yes, I did. Because …

Balnick looked at Tenuto as though he needed help. Tenuto was not looking at Balnick. He was looking into the opposite corner of the room, with a hand cupped over his right ear. We found out later that Tenuto was hard of hearing and he usually turned his good ear to the witness so he could hear what was going on. Uncertainly, Balnick resumed.

BALNICK: Because the labor—she was an elderly prima gravida. Labor was not progressing.

BILL: Are you now saying, sir, that she was in labor throughout the night and that is why you ordered the X-ray, because the labor was not effective?

BALNICK: Not necessarily for that reason only.

BILL: Doctor, minutes ago you testified that an X-ray was ordered because labor was not progressing.

BALNICK: Yes, and I add to that, because even if she wouldn't have been in labor—admitted to the hospital as an elderly prima gravida—with her head still high, still gets an X-ray pelvimetry.

The "her" Balnick referred to was, of course, Heather. The concern of the hospital staff about the position of the fetus's head was noted in the hospital records.

> BILL: Again, were the X-rays ordered because the labor was ineffectual?
>
> BALNICK: No.
>
> BILL: In any event, was not the pelvimetry done to determine whether or not the baby was going to be born spontaneously?
>
> BALNICK: The question cannot be answered yes or no.
>
> JUDGE: Just answer the question. If you don't understand it, tell Mr. Dugan so.
>
> BALNICK: Yes, Lorraine was in ineffectual labor and an X-ray showed a cephalopelvic disproportion.
>
> BILL: And then, would one not do a Caesarian section?
>
> BALNICK: Yes. Right away.
>
> BILL: Right away? Doctor, if one delays a Caesarian section after having that information, that could very well lead to fetal distress, is that correct?
>
> BALNICK: Yes, Mr. Dugan.
>
> BILL: And fetal distress could lead to hypoxia, a complete deprivation of oxygen to the brain, which could result in severe brain damage, if it went on long enough. Is that correct?
>
> BALNICK: Yes, it could.
>
> BILL: Mr. Tenuto has told the jury that you crossed out "CPD," the abbreviation for cephalopelvic disproportion, in the hospital records. Did you do that sir?
>
> BALNICK: Yes, I did. I crossed it out wherever it was mentioned.

BILL: When Mr. Tenuto showed the cross-outs to you, did he ask you what was underneath them?

BALNICK: I found them inaccurate.

JUDGE: The lawyer is asking you "Did Mr. Tenuto discuss these things with you?"

BILL: Yes. I am trying to figure out when it came into your consciousness that there were "CPD" underneath those cross-outs?

BALNICK: When I studied the case.

BILL: Perhaps you have been told about people taking copies of the hospital records, and handwriting experts looking at them? Perhaps you have been told about those experts before they figured out you had crossed out "CPD?"

BALNICK: Well, I don't have any individual recollection about this case. It was ten, eleven years ago. All I can go is after the record. I was with the hospital for three years.

O'NEILL: Objection. Dr. Balnick's answer is beyond the parameters of the question.

JUDGE: Sustained.

BILL: Dr. Balnick, again, did you cross out "CPD?"

BALNICK: I ...

Balnick looked sheepishly at Tenuto, but Tenuto was still not looking at him.

JUDGE: Say yes or no, Doctor. The jury is listening, sir.

BALNICK: It was "CPD" I crossed out.

BILL: What was the usual procedure at the hospital? Was it not that a doctor would look at all the available records and write a final summary?

BALNICK: Yes.

BILL: If an X-ray were taken, it would be part of the record. Not only that, a radiologist would review the X-ray and make a report. The X-ray and the report would go into the record?

BALNICK: That is true. But I never saw an X-ray report.

O'NEILL: Move to strike the answer.

TENUTO: He is only talking in general, Doctor.

JUDGE: Denied.

BILL: The resident who wrote "fetal distress" and "CPD" in the final report must have gotten it somewhere. Where are the X-rays and the X-ray report?

BALNICK: I don't know where the report is. I have never seen the X-ray.

BILL: Are you telling this jury, sir, that without an X-ray, without an X-ray report, you distinctly remember and have a distinct recollection there was no cephalopelvic disproportion?

BALNICK: I am telling you that I was informed verbally.

This answer set off a long, loud exchange between the three attorneys. Judge James finally ruled that Balnick could answer Bill's question about seeing or being told about the X-ray. His answer, however, did not have a binding effect on the hospital, the judge said.

BALNICK: I am telling you that I was informed verbally. This is a customary procedure. It is also done when I order an X-ray pelvimetry. Certainly within an hour or two hours after the X-ray pelvimetry has been taken, I was informed if there was a cephalopelvic disproportion, in which case I would have returned to the hospital. Otherwise, they would have thrown me out of the hospital and the chief would have delivered the patient.

At O'Neill's insistence, after another noisy exchange between the attorneys, Judge James told the jury the answer "doesn't have any binding effect upon the hospital in respect to what they would have done or might have done."

BILL: Let's move on to another item of "correct" testimony. In 1975, at the EBT, you said you were at the hospital at 3:30 PM. Your testimony was not true, was it, sir?

BALNICK: No, it was misinformed.

BILL: Just answer the question. That testimony wasn't true.

BALNICK: I arrived at seven o'—

TENUTO (shouting): I object to the word "true!"

BILL (also shouting): "True" is what I said, and "true" is what I mean.

TENUTO: Then I object to it.

JUDGE: He can answer.

BILL: The testimony about examining Mrs. Zarecor every hour after 3:30 was also untrue.

Bill may have meant to ask a question, but his tone was now angry and demanding. Balnick had been shrinking back into his chair, but now leaned forward, as if to confront Bill. He changed his posture in this way several times during his testimony, but always seemed to reconsider the confrontational position and would return to the shrinking position. It was clearly a difficult position for Balnick to be in—being accused of lying, and being unable to refute the accusation.

BALNICK: It wasn't correct.

BILL: Did you ever once in the last four years attempt to correct it and go to the Zarecors and say, "Wait a minute, all of that testimony I gave was incorrect"?

BALNICK: Nobody … nobody … contacted me.

BILL: Did you only decide to tell the truth when Mr. Tenuto informed you of all the experts being assembled to prove you were lying?

TENUTO: (He was red in the face and shouting) I strenuously object! I have done nothing improper!

For several minutes, Bill, Balnick, Tenuto, and O'Neill were shouting simultaneously. Tenuto and O'Neill demanded one more time that a mistrial be declared. Balnick was addressing angry comments to Bill, giving up his shrinking act and showing real anger and hostility. Bill was saying Balnick had changed his testimony radically and we should know "when he saw the light."

In the midst of all the shouting and demands, Judge James suddenly covered his mouth with a hand and jumped up. "I have new caps and they are coming out!" he cried over the din. "Excuse me, please." He ran out of the courtroom, instructing the clerk of the court, "Please let the jury out for a short recess."

There was no more testimony that day. The judge had to pay his dentist an emergency visit.

"Gee, that was exciting," Lorraine said, as we were leaving. "I wonder if they are going to shout and carry on that way for the whole trial?"

TWENTY-SEVEN

When I arrived to hear the second day of testimony, Bill was standing outside the courtroom with a well-dressed man in a blue suit. Bill introduced me to Dr. Seymour Kane, our expert witness on the birth. Balnick had not finished his testimony, but since Dr. Kane could only testify the next day, all the attorneys agreed Balnick could finish his testimony later.

Lorraine had been sent by Bill to see Kane, and she liked him very much. "I get the feeling he wants to tear Balnick to pieces," she told me. "He didn't say much, but he was clearly upset with what he found in the hospital records."

Bill and Kane were talking about running. Bill had run ten miles for the first time the day before. "I don't think it's a good idea," Kane said. "The benefits are not all some would lead you to believe."

"Ken wouldn't agree with you, Doctor. Would you, Ken?" Bill said, referring to the fact I had recently run about fifty pounds off my body.

"No," I answered. "I don't agree with Dr. Kane. But he can have his opinion. What does a doctor know, anyway?"

We all laughed together.

When Kane took the witness stand, he gave his name and address and answered the standard questions about being licensed to practice medicine in New York State. He told Bill he had testified for and against defendants in malpractice suits. Kane listed associations with four New York City hospitals, and he had the highest rank possible for a part-time teacher at a local medical college, teaching clinical obstetrics and gynecology.

Bill and Kane went through the doctor's qualifications for nearly twenty minutes. Finally, after Judge James had commented on the length of time being taken just to establish Kane's credentials, Bill got to the point.

> BILL: Doctor, did you, at the request of our office, review certain records for the purposes of rendering an opinion in this case?
>
> KANE: Yes. I reviewed the hospital's obstetrical records, the hospital's newborn records, and University Hospital's records.

Because University Hospital sent microfilm copies of their records, Judge James would not allow Bill to use them. All of Kane's testimony was based on the records of the hospital where Heather was born.

> BILL: Let me remind the jury that Mrs. Zarecor was an "elderly prima gravida"—a woman thirty-seven years of age, having her first child. Would you tell us what significance that fact has to a doctor?
>
> KANE: She is at significantly greater risk for complications of the pregnancy and delivery. It is fundamental, something even an intern or resident would know.

Kane narrated the story of the birth, reading from the nurse's notes in the hospital records, making comments. Lorraine was admitted at ten o'clock on March 26, 1969. She gave an antecedent history of having started labor three hours earlier, at seven o'clock. The hospital staff examined her and found she was one finger dilated and having moderate contractions. They admitted her in early labor. The cervix would have to dilate five fingers before the baby could pass through, Kane added.

Shortly after admission, Lorraine had a "bloody show," an expulsion of the mucus and blood inside the mouth of the womb. This was further evidence of the progression of the process of labor. At 12:45 AM, the patient had dilated another finger. She was now two fingers dilated. Shortly thereafter, the contractions were strong and occurring every three minutes.

At 1:45 AM, there was another "good bloody show." An intern was notified. He found the fluid, which surrounds the baby, "has no leakage."

The nurse's notes indicated Lorraine "felt like pushing with the contractions." This more or less alerted the people caring for her that perhaps delivery was imminent. The intern continued to examine Lorraine and the nurses to note the timing of the contractions, the fetal heartbeat, and conditions of the membranes. The membranes stayed intact; the contractions become frequent and strong. The fetal heartbeat was noted as being normal.

At 7:20 AM, March 27, Lorraine was taken to the X-ray department for a pelvimetry.

Bill broke into Kane's narration at this point:

> BILL: Doctor, with reasonable medical certainty, was Mrs. Zarecor in labor during the period of time about which you have just given testimony— from 10:00 PM until 7:20 AM?
>
> KANE: There is no question she was definitely in labor, as evidenced by the notation of continuing contractions that are described variously as either moderate or strong. Also, she did dilate progressively from one finger on admission to two fingers. Dr. Balnick's contention, in 1975, under oath, was that she was not in labor during this period. I find that is contrary to fact.
>
> BILL: Meaning?
>
> KANE: Mrs. Zarecor was clearly in labor, but it was definitely a desultory labor, or an ineffectual type of labor.
>
> BILL: And to further clarify for the jury—
>
> KANE: The labor did not achieve various milestones of progress one would reasonably anticipate. Because the milestones of progressive dilation of the cervix and the engagement of the fetal head were not achieved, it is absolutely appropriate for someone to order an X-ray pelvimetry to investigate the problem.
>
> BILL: Would you tell us what an X-ray pelvimetry is?
>
> KANE: An X-ray pelvimetry is a group of X-rays taken to determine the size and exact physical dimension of the pelvis. A small pelvis may account for lack of progress. The concept is that nature, in her wisdom, is never bent on self-destruction. If labor is relatively arrested or ineffectual, this is nature's way of saying there may be a problem.
>
> BILL: Is there a shorthand term that could indicate an abnormal condition?

KANE: Yes. It is "CPD." It stands for cephalopelvic disproportion.

BILL: Do a woman's pelvic measurements ever change?

KANE: No. They will change only if the woman is elderly and has severe arthritis.

BILL: Well, as everyone knows, the X-rays at the hospital are missing. The solution was simple and obvious—have X-rays taken of Lorraine's pelvis.

Bill, with a dramatic flourish that would have done credit to any dramatist in the world, offered X-rays Kane had ordered taken of Lorraine into evidence. O'Neill and Tenuto both looked surprised. O'Neill jumped up, raised his hand, and opened his mouth as if about to say something. Instead, he simply shook his head, smiled, and sat down. Neither man objected to admitting the X-rays into evidence. Tenuto sat with his mouth closed, but with his jaw moving. I wondered if he was cursing Bill under his breath or gnashing his teeth. The X-rays became plaintiff's exhibit number 4. An X-ray report was attached. In a few short minutes, Bill managed to repeat several times that the original X-ray and X-ray report were missing.

Before discussing the X-rays and the report, Bill asked for an expert opinion on the care Lorraine had received up to the time the hospital ordered X-rays.

BILL: Doctor, do you have an opinion, based upon reasonable medical certainty, as to whether there were any departures on the part of Dr. Balnick—or the hospital—from accepted standards as they existed in 1969?

KANE: I feel the hospital had committed two conspicuous departures from accepted standards. First, the records indicated only one blood pressure was taken in ten hours and twenty-five minutes. Secondly, no admission urinalysis was taken. When a urinalysis was taken, it indicated significant protein in the urine. The presence of protein in the urine may signal the development of toxemia—toxemia of pregnancy. Elevated blood pressure may also indicate toxemia.

BILL: Would you also explain this, Doctor?

KANE: Toxemia of pregnancy means, simply, a complication of pregnancy. It represents dual jeopardy to the mother and the infant. Persistence of high blood pressure means the child is not getting a full complement of oxygen. This is a constriction of blood vessels all over the body. The child is not getting the usual amount of oxygen. The eventual effect of getting less oxygen could be brain damage to the child.

BILL: And how should this situation be handled?

KANE: The hospital should absolutely have informed Dr. Balnick that a toxemia of pregnancy had developed. Balnick should have given his immediate attention to the matter. This condition mandates prompt intervention. The uterus should be emptied by whatever means necessary, such as Caesarian section, as quickly as feasible in the interest of the mother and the infant. Failure to do so can certainly do neither any good.

BILL: The records indicate that Heather Zarecor was born with a very low Apgar score. Would you explain what an Apgar score is, Doctor?

KANE: When a child is delivered, it is evaluated at two time intervals—after one minute of life and at five minutes of life. There are five aspects one looks at in order to come to a conclusion about the health and well-being of the infant. The five categories are: color of the baby, respiratory effort, how limp or active the baby is, the heart rate of the baby, the cry and response to stimuli. If a child is perfect, it will be given a ten. If a child is dead, it will be given a score of zero.

BILL: And Heather's score?

KANE: Heather had an Apgar score of two at one minute of life. This is an extremely grave situation. At five minutes of life, Heather's Apgar score had gone up to three. However, she was still in very grave condition.

BILL: Would you elaborate?

KANE: There was certainly a contributory effect, between the deviation from standard medical care for a pregnant woman in 1969 and the eventual Apgar score of two. Other factors are involved. One of the other factors included the fact the fetal head was not engaged. If a baby's head is not engaged, one should be alerted to the fact there may be a problem. The doctors should have considered the possibility that something was wrong with Lorraine's pelvis.

BILL: Do you find anything else abnormal about the record?

KANE: One of the alterations in the hospital record made by Dr. Balnick indicates Heather's head was engaged just before he did the Caesarian. A nurse's note at 7:10 PM, about an hour before Heather was born, said, however, "presenting part not engaged." If the presenting part—the head—was not engaged at 7:10 PM, it would never have been engaged. The alteration in the hospital record was totally inconsistent with the nurse's notes, and the truth as constructed from the balance of the record.

Bill and Kane established the connection between the nurse's notes and examinations by the intern at 3:30 AM and 7 AM. Balnick originally claimed he did these examinations in the afternoon hours. He had since admitted he could not have done them. The jury was told and retold about this "error."

KANE: After Lorraine was taken into the X-ray department, "blood was sent to the laboratory for cross-matching for transfusion and RH typing," according to the hospital record. The only reason blood would be cross-matched in an obstetrical case [other than for severe anemia, which Lorraine did suffer], would be to have it in readiness for surgery. Obviously, the only surgery contemplated for Lorraine could have been a Caesarian section.

One more piece fell into place:

KANE: If any X-ray pelvimetry showed CPD, the hospital staff would have been acting properly and wisely to prepare for any contingency in an operation. The blood would have to be cross-matched in case a transfusion was needed. If the cephalopelvic disproportion did exist, time is of the essence so that the fetus is not brain-damaged, because of the lack of oxygen.

BILL: Was there a CPD?

KANE: On the basis of my own clinical examination, and Lorraine's X-rays, there is a total documentation indicating this patient has a pelvis that is critically small in certain pivotal areas. Unequivocally, the pelvis size is compromised.

Judge James did not like the "artistic" use of the word "compromised."

KANE: I mean it is a deviation from what you would expect to see in a normal-sized pelvis.

Also at the judge's prompting, Kane allowed that Lorraine's pelvic measurements were "unusually smaller" than normal. Neither Tenuto nor O'Neill objected to Kane's descriptions. While I understood that the judge was trying to give the jury as clear and accurate a picture of the birth process as possible, I wondered why the two defense attorneys did not do that, if only to protect their clients. The answer in my own mind was that they did not have a basic understanding of the case they were trying.

KANE: The differences between the X-rays now in the courtroom and those taken in 1969 are that the new ones had no baby in them. Even though the baby in the X-ray in 1969 is small, the only safe, sane way to deliver it, after the information obtained by taking the X-ray was available, would be by Caesarian section. Anyone can deliver a child vaginally, but it is really the condition of the delivered child that is crucial. It has happened that children have been delivered in the face of a disproportion, but the likelihood is overwhelming it is going to have brain damage.

BILL: Doctor, what should have been done?

KANE: Even if Dr. Balnick had not been told of the results of the pelvimetry, it was his obligation to find out what the X-ray had yielded in terms of information. During the day, the hospital noted two increases in Lorraine's blood pressure. They should have done more than just note it. They should have notified Dr. Balnick.

BILL: Let's get back now to the events of the pregnancy.

KANE: All right. Throughout the day, more examinations are

made by interns or residents. At six o'clock there is a significant finding—the most significant—a meconium staining is seen.

BILL: Why? In your opinion, what events lead up to the meconium staining?

Up to this point, Kane had been cool, somewhat detached. Now, as he spoke, his voice took on a biting edge. His jaw tightened and he seemed to be forcing the words out.

KANE: I think it is very clear. By six o'clock, Lorraine had been in labor twenty-three hours, an inordinately long time in 1969. It was an especially long time given all the evidence of lack of progress and toxemia of pregnancy. I think you must consider the fact the stress of the protracted labor in the presence of some type of disproportion, coupled with toxemia of pregnancy, had ultimately taken its toll in terms of injuring this child, depriving this child of oxygen, and then subsequently being evidence of meconium. The hospital records document more signs of fetal distress. First, the fetal heart slows down, and then it becomes irregular. Finally, severe meconium staining was observed. Obviously, this was an emergency situation that should have been avoided.

BILL: How?

KANE: Even with the signs of fetal distress, Lorraine could and should have been better treated. The hospital could have done two simple things. They could have, first, given her oxygen. The staff, apparently, brought oxygen into the labor room, but never used it. This simple, no-risk step would have allowed Lorraine to breathe ninety-eight to ninety-nine percent pure oxygen, instead of the nineteen percent she was breathing in the room. It would have saturated the maternal blood with oxygen, thus giving more to the fetus, particularly to the baby's brain.

BILL: What else?

KANE: The hospital staff should also have turned Lorraine on her side. The weight of the pregnant uterus rests on the main blood-collecting system in the body when the woman is on her back. This impedes the return of the blood to the heart. On her side, the heart receives as much blood as the person can supply to be pumped. Both procedures are harmless. The hospital staff should have done them. They were in use in 1969 and many years before that.

BILL: Suppose there had been no X-ray pelvimetry. Would that excuse the results of Lorraine's pregnancy?

KANE: With or without an X-ray, the appropriate course of action was to do a Caesarian section certainly early in the morning, on the basis of failure to progress, her age, the fact it was her first pregnancy, and the fact she had developed toxemia. To subject this patient to protracted labor, on top of what she had already been through, was the last straw in causing a progressive deterioration of the infant's condition.

BILL: With a reasonable medical certainty, Doctor, do you have an opinion as to whether these departures from accepted practice, as they existed in 1969, were a competent producing cause of Heather Zarecor's condition, as it exists today?

KANE: Yes, I have. They were.

The information Kane and Bill developed during the day could hardly be expected to make easy listening. I felt as though I had been in the courtroom thirty years. I felt again the kind of fatigue I felt while waiting to see if Heather would survive at all. I had wanted this information for nearly eleven years. Finally getting it did not make me feel better.

You can live with a situation like this and deal with it, but you never really get over it. The Bible says if you know the truth, it shall make you free. Not really. Certainly not in this case. When it is the kind of truth revealed by Bill and Dr. Kane from the hospital records, a truth that revealed how senseless this whole accident was, it can make the pain you bear heavier and more intolerable.

TWENTY-EIGHT

Lorraine and I had a quiet, depressed lunch together. She said she would not stay for the afternoon session. She'd heard all she could take for one day.

I finished eating and walked Lorraine to the subway and then went looking for Steve and Bill. They had spent the lunch recess going over points to be covered in redirect examination by Bill after O'Neill and Tenuto had cross-examined Kane. "I think you may get a bit of comic relief, Ken," Bill said. "I really don't think those two are up for going after Kane."

Like Lorraine, I would have been happy to end the session and come back another day. Bill, however, was in a good mood. Actually, he was closer to elated. As we walked back to the courtroom, he asked me twice if I thought the jury got all the points he made. "I know you did," he said. "I can also see in your face you find the whole thing deeply, deeply disturbing."

"Of course I'm upset," I said. "And what I have real trouble accepting is the fact that it seems to have been totally unnecessary. Surely there was somebody in that bunch that cared … or knew, or could take charge … or …"

"I know," Steve interrupted. "Sadly there was not."

Bill and Steve joked about how flat-footed both O'Neill and Tenuto had appeared when the X-ray was introduced into evidence. "The defense doesn't have any kind of case," Bill said. "Maybe these two will throw in the towel soon."

When we got back into the courtroom, Judge James was on the bench, waiting to begin. Dr. Kane was also waiting. At Judge James's request, I went down the hall to fetch O'Neill and Tenuto from a small conference room where they were meeting.

O'Neill questioned Kane first, and was quick to arouse the doctor's anger. Kane told O'Neill he had testified in thirteen or fifteen medical malpractice cases in the past ten years. He said, rather testily, his income was "basically derived from the practice of medicine." O'Neill kept hammering away about Kane's testimony in malpractice cases, trying, I assume, to get the jury to believe that Kane would give any opinion in any case if he were paid for it. *Well, you don't have to be smart to be dirty*, I thought.

O'Neill then went for the familiar. No, Dr. Kane told him under questioning, he had not been in the hospital when these events took place. Yes, his testimony was based on his reading of the records left by the men and women who had been there. Yes, Kane agreed with O'Neill that labor normally causes pain, and pain, in turn, can elevate blood pressure. "But not to certain critical levels," Kane added. "Mrs. Zarecor's blood pressure had reached critical levels."

During O'Neill's questioning, Kane displayed less and less tolerance of both O'Neill and his questions. O'Neill made errors throughout the trial, to ascribe a benevolent cause to the behavior, based on misreading, or a failure of careful and thorough study of the record. Kane frequently corrected O'Neill's errors. Finally, O'Neill blew up.

> O'NEILL: Mrs. Zarecor was sleeping between contractions at three o'clock.
>
> KANE: I don't know how you concluded that. The record indicates she slept at 11:50 AM. The three o'clock entry was something totally different.
>
> O'NEILL: I ask the questions! That is the game we play! I ask the questions!

In spite of the frequent and, I would have thought, embarrassing corrections, O'Neill continued to read the 11:50 AM and 3:00 PM entries as a single entry. Kane did not give up either: the handwritings are different, he pointed out to O'Neill. O'Neill impatiently drummed his fingers on the table, "Doctor," he demanded, "in addition to your other training, did you take a course in handwriting?"

A resident or intern could not have done the Caesarian without the presence of the attending physician, Kane said. It was the attending physician's,

Balnick's, responsibility. Having scored at least one point for the hospital, O'Neill chose to go to another subject.

> O'NEILL: Doctor, were you told Heather Zarecor was a microcephalic?

Bill laughed out loud and shook his head. Both the judge and O'Neill shot hostile looks his way, but here was yet another error. If O'Neill truly believed Heather was microcephalic at birth, he had not done his homework, or did not have a clue as to the meaning of entries in the hospital records. Heather's head was normal-sized when she was born. It has not grown normally during her life, but that is a result of the damage done at birth, not because of a congenital problem. After O'Neill's distortions came to be a frequently recurring phenomenon, I began to wonder if he was doing it on purpose, hoping to confuse the jury.

When it was established what microcephalic means—it is a head that is smaller-than-normal in size, in relation to the rest of the body—O'Neill was through.

Tenuto now had a turn at Dr. Kane. He would be brief, he said, and he was. He asked if meconium staining could, or would, possibly indicate something other than fetal distress. Kane replied, "Possibly, but it is a warning sign."

Tenuto also got Kane to agree there was nothing in the record to indicate Balnick was informed by the hospital of the happenings of the day. Tenuto, having made a point against the hospital, smiled and sat down. He was through with this witness.

On redirect, Bill got Kane to read Balnick's office record entry about Lorraine:

"3/26/69, admitted hospital, false labor, started mild, desultory labor, 3/27." After reading that entry, Kane added, "This is not consistent with the rest of the record."

Under further questioning, Kane added, "Heather was in good condition when the X-ray was taken and the blood was cross-matched. If the Caesarian had been done then, I don't believe this child would have been damaged. The deterioration took place subsequent to that time. Dr. Balnick's failure to appear was an absolute departure from the accepted medical standards existing in 1969. Balnick's failure to appear was a clear competent producing cause of this baby's problem today."

Bill and I were both pleased to see Kane had stood up so well to O'Neill. Tenuto had not tried to challenge him, and O'Neill's challenge had been, in my opinion, kind of feeble. O'Neill had made few points, mainly a minor one when he got Kane to agree the interns could not have performed the Caesarian. That put more of the blame at Balnick's door, but Tenuto had also made a point that there were no entries in the record that hospital staff had tried to inform Balnick of events as they spiraled into disaster. Plus, the chief of service at the hospital could have intervened and performed a Caesarian, and this point would be made later.

As I reflected later, I would have preferred to have Kane show a little more tolerance of O'Neill. Not that I thought this lawyer deserved kindness, nor did I think he was doing an adequate job representing his client, but I did not want the jury to feel our witness was arrogant.

Kane was dismissed and Balnick would be back on the stand tomorrow. When he was through, I would testify.

Though I was happy with the way the trial was going, I was bothered by the animosity between Bill and Tenuto. Exchanges between them on the simplest subject nearly always degenerated into exchanges that were loud, angry, and needlessly long. What they thought of each other, personally or professionally, did not concern me, but I did think it would be senseless for this case to drag on and on only because the two of them could not, or would not, talk to each other in a civil manner. I had Lorraine call Ron Tuscano and suggest that maybe he could deal with Tenuto—or better, with the insurance company that was paying Tenuto. Lorraine told me that Ron had told her Steve had talked to him about the same subject, and he understood our concerns.

Ron was sitting in the public section of Judge James's courtroom when I arrived to hear the next day of testimony. Lorraine's call had prompted him to "show his face," and hopefully get a chance to talk to Tenuto and O'Neill. He also wanted to talk to me about matters concerning the case.

Ron had used our concern about the relationship between Bill and Tenuto to make a call to Balnick's insurance carrier. He told them he was available to talk any time they felt like talking. The company's response was to say Tenuto had exclusive control of the case as long as the trial lasted. They would, however, make an approach to Tenuto to see if he needed or wanted help or "guidance."

At this time, both Tenuto and O'Neill entered the courtroom, so Ron led me out and down the hall. "How do you think the case is going, Ken?" Ron asked.

"I think we're doing extremely well," I said, wondering if this was a question Bill had prompted. "Balnick will be back on the stand soon, and I want Bill to ask him point-blank why he did not come to the hospital. He had not been ill and there was no accident. But this one time, the only time in his entire career, as far as we can determine, he abrogated his responsibility. I'm willing to bet he knows why he was not there."

Balnick was talking to Bill when Ron and I reentered the courtroom. Judge James was on the bench, as usual, waiting for everyone to get into place. We were scheduled to start at ten. It was nearly half past. The trial never started at the advertised times. I always arrived twenty to thirty minutes late, and never missed a word of testimony.

When the four attorneys were in place, Bill asked Balnick to be seated in the witness stand. Bill requested permission to put a statement on the record, before the jury was brought back into the courtroom. Judge James granted permission for Bill to speak.

"Prior to the start of the trial," Bill said, "the defendants in the action had been informed we would settle for 1.2 million. It was not a bargaining figure; it was our final offer. The figure was based on our anticipation that we could get a verdict in excess of two million dollars, and on the fact that we have seen a recent Appellate Division decision that upheld a verdict as high as 1.5 million. In my humble opinion, jury verdicts should not be disturbed, but they are, and I have so informed the Zarecors."

Bill spoke at length, putting on record our intention to collect every penny of the verdict we got that the Appellate Division upheld. This could mean collecting money directly from Balnick. Balnick carried one million dollars in insurance; the hospital had a policy in the amount of two million. "If our verdict places two-thirds responsibility for negligence on Dr. Balnick, and one-third on the hospital," Bill said, looking directly at Balnick, "we would collect one-point-four million from the doctor's carrier. He would be exposed for $400,000. If Dr. Balnick is held liable in this case alone by the jury, his exposure would be much more."

In other words, Balnick might have to pay the part of the judgment that exceeded the amount of his coverage from his private funds. As Bill spoke, his message to Balnick became clearer and clearer: You had better do something to cover your ass, sweetheart. 'Cause if you don't, it'll be sore the rest of your life ...

In conclusion, Bill made two points. "After today, we will not accept or offer a settlement of one million two. Second, I know from Mr. Tenuto that he has Dr. Balnick's consent to settle the case. The only question is the amount. We submit the failure to pay the full amount of Dr. Balnick's policy constitutes bad faith. If Dr. Balnick is hit for a verdict or exposed to a verdict over one million dollars, he might have a right to look to the carrier for reimbursement for that amount."

Before Tenuto could respond to Bill, Balnick, who had been fidgeting nervously all the time Bill talked, blurted out, "I don't have any assets."

"Don't say anything, Doctor," Judge James cautioned.

"Your Honor, we're dealing with something of an unusual procedure here," Tenuto said as he stood up. "But I have no objection to having everything in the open. I have informed Dr. Balnick of everything Bill—Mr. Dugan—has said. We're in contact every day. We now offer to settle the case by paying one half of the $750,000 the insurance company feels the case is worth. There is, however, still disagreement with the hospital's carrier. That insurance company doesn't feel they should pay half of any settlement."

"No," Bill said. "It is obvious the carrier is acting in bad faith. I think the bad faith in this case is disgraceful, and I will not renew my offer to settle this case in this manner beyond today."

That is as far as it went. The settlement discussion was over. Bill smiled, Tenuto looked grim, O'Neill was clearly annoyed, and Balnick looked apprehensive as he sat and squirmed in the witness box. They jury was brought in, and Judge James reminded Balnick that he had been sworn in previously.

Bill opened by reminding Balnick of his previous testimony. They would use Balnick's terms to characterize his 1975 testimony, Bill said. Balnick had admitted in open court his previous testimony was "mistaken." These "mistakes" seemed to be causing Balnick some agitation.

> BILL: How did it come about that you remembered you were mistaken?
>
> BALNICK: Looking at the nurse's notes.

BILL: The nurse's notes are the most complete notes in the hospital record?

BALNICK: Yes.

BILL: And the nurses at the scene record only what they are told—told by the doctors, told by the interns. They make accurate records?

BALNICK: Yes.

This was not the Balnick who had angrily confronted Bill previously. He continually squirmed and smiled sheepishly at Bill as he answered the questions.

BILL: Doctor, was there a CPD?

BALNICK: Well, I …

And so on. Finally, Bill had admitted into evidence Balnick's office records, and Balnick admitted his notation about Lorraine being admitted "in false labor" in those records was "factually inaccurate."

When Bill had finished with Balnick, O'Neill took his turn to question the doctor. O'Neill established that Balnick could not specifically remember ordering the X-ray or talking to the hospital staff concerning Lorraine's condition.

BALNICK: I can only go by what the usual procedure is. A patient is not forgotten. The doctor is notified about the progress.

O'NEILL: Dr. Balnick, were you at another hospital on March 27, 1969? Did you have an affiliation with another hospital?

BALNICK: I did. But I cannot remember being there, and I cannot remember having office hours that day.

O'NEILL: All right, Doctor. Getting back to Heather Zarecor. Was she microcephalic at birth?

BALNICK: I don't know.

O'Neill is truly incredible, I thought. This lawyer will not get off this error, even after Dr. Kane had explained it and argued with him about it.

After Balnick was made to repeat one more time that his 1975 testimony "was a mistake," O'Neill sat down. It was Tenuto's turn to question his client.

I was wondering if he understood the records any better than O'Neill did. I still don't know.

> TENUTO: It just so happens, that at this time I have no questions for Dr. Balnick. I will reserve the right, of course, to recall him as part of my own case.

Balnick was excused by the judge. He hurriedly grabbed his coat and the pretty young lady who had accompanied him, and left the courtroom. He didn't say good-bye to his counsel or anyone else.

Bill called me to the witness stand. I spent several hours sitting in the witness chair, but most of the time was taken listening to the attorneys bicker about my testimony. It seems I could not answer more than one or two questions without O'Neill or Tenuto, usually both, standing up and objecting. When Bill would respond to them, they would shout even louder, frequently ending with a demand that a mistrial be declared.

O'Neill, especially, objected to my "colorful" and "dramatic" descriptions. When I recounted being told by a doctor at University Hospital that Balnick "fucked this one up," their howls reached a crescendo pitch. Although their demands for a mistrial had just been denied less than five minutes before, first O'Neill, and then Tenuto, demanded a mistrial. Judge James was having none of it.

> JUDGE: Motion denied. This is part of a spontaneous declaration of this witness, who, I tell you, is apparently, or was then, apparently, talking and reacting under the impact of a very traumatic and startling event. To prevent him from stating the things he did and the things he said, under the circumstances, when his child is near death, would be to deprive the jury of an opportunity to understand the man. You have the right and opportunity to cross-examine him in regard to what he said. I have taken to be what I consider "prophylactic measures" with respect to the statement, which I could not anticipate he would make, though I would again, authorize him to go ahead under the circumstances. Even had I known, I would nevertheless have permitted him to make the statement of his behavior, conversations and reactions during this very difficult time in his life.

I could not have agreed more, but even this statement by the judge did not keep O'Neill from frequent, loud objections as I continued my testimony. He got really upset when I started crying. Truly, I would rather not have cried on the witness stand, but the thought of Lorraine and Heather suffering brought all those scenes back to life and upset me more than ever. Now that I knew for certain how needless all of that suffering was, the pain was even more real.

O'Neill objected to my testimony concerning some of the medical experts we had taken Heather to. He objected on the grounds that I was offering expert testimony, testimony I was not qualified to give. Bill told the court that my testimony would be corroborated by medical testimony.

O'NEILL (Speaking very loudly): Then let the doctors testify! Why put this man through it?

Bill did not directly answer that question, but said I should tell the jury, before I finished, "the highlights of your life with Heather." I started, getting through all the painful details without tears. "Heather has no concept of where she is. It is apparent whenever you speak to her, or whenever a light goes on, or a noise is made, that you are interfering in her own private darkness, because she will jump or react in a frightened way. She is in a darkness of her own. Whenever you touch her, you pull her out of it."

O'Neill objected, complaining that I was offering testimony that was a question of medical proof. He said what I said was "highly prejudicial."

Judge James was truly impartial in this trial, but it was also clear from his facial expressions that some of what was being said was affecting him. When O'Neill said my testimony was "highly prejudicial," the judge's eyes widened and he leaned back in his chair as he looked down and directly at O'Neill as he spoke. "The use of the term 'she lives in her own dark, private world,' is colorful, but hardly inaccurate, if she is brain-damaged. Are you contending she is not?"

The judge looked at O'Neill for a few seconds. O'Neill mumbled a timid, "No, Your Honor," and sat down. The judge then turned his gaze on Tenuto. There was no response from Tenuto either, so the judge continued.

"What he did to find out about Heather's condition and how he tried to help her are always subject to cross-examination and to proof, to refute them. They are not matters beyond the power of the defendant to deal with. For the father of this child to have done less, it seems to me, may have a bearing on his credibility, and may have a bearing on his right to recover anything."

I resumed my testimony, but was interrupted again when I started to explain about checking institutions for Heather. O'Neill objected on the grounds that this information should come through medical testimony. Judge James told O'Neill, before Bill could respond to his latest objection, that my testimony was subject to "connection." Bill agreed all of my testimony would be connected. "That cannot be," O'Neill said as he shook his head. "They have not institutionalized her. How can it be connected?"

This statement drew a furious response from Bill. He turned red, pounded the table, and pointed a finger at O'Neill. Bill shouted, "You better believe this child has been at home all this time. And you are going to hear why she has been home all of this time and not been institutionalized!"

Tenuto, who had said very little all day long, now joined O'Neill's objection and the loud arguments started all over. Judge James, in exasperation, finally suggested we close for the day and let our experts testify. I could be "recalled after them." Bill agreed. The trial was adjourned for the day.

I was called two more times to the witness stand. Both times I didn't do much testifying, but mostly listened as arguments about my testimony continued. Eventually, however, I was able to tell my story, pretty much as I wanted to tell it. Why O'Neill chose to challenge virtually every sentence I uttered is beyond me. Steve may have had the most logical explanation: "You are, in this situation, a sympathetic character, and maybe they are trying to make your testimony look exaggerated or overdramatic. Of course, by objecting to everything you say, he is only highlighting it. This doesn't help him achieve his goal, I would say."

Four witnesses made the rest of our case. The first was a wonderful old man, Joseph Winreb, who ran the largest private association for aid to the retarded in New York State. Winreb told the court it would cost about $75,000 a year to set up a home facility for Heather. He added it would be difficult, if not impossible, to "place" a child in Heather's condition. In any case, keeping her home was the most humane and healthiest choice to make. Heather would live longer and better at home, he said.

Just before Lorraine took the witness stand, Heather was brought into the courtroom and shown to the jury. Bill wanted us to make her laugh. Lorraine and I both made her favorite noises and Bill talked to her, but Heather did nothing but ignore the whole thing.

I have often wondered what the jury thought when they saw Heather.

Many people who see her, or who see any obviously retarded person, seem embarrassed, frightened, or upset. Several of the jurors, whose eyes showed life as they listened to other testimony, seemed to have blank looks. One juror, a woman who seemed to be by far the oldest person on the panel, raised a hand as if reaching out to help me when I took Heather from her wheelchair. I do not know if the reactions were shock, sadness, anger, revulsion, or what.

After Heather had been shown to the jury, Lorraine took the witness stand. After pro forma questioning by Bill, Tenuto immediately launched into an attack on her. It was one of the dumbest episodes of the trial.

Lorraine had lied about her age when she went to Planned Parenthood. Tenuto waved the application, which had been part of Balnick's office records, in Lorraine's face. Balnick knew her true age when she was under his care during the pregnancy. He had testified to that fact during the examination before trial and under questioning at the trial by Bill. Nonetheless, minutes after the jury had seen Heather and the results of Balnick's negligence, Tenuto tried to embarrass Lorraine and get her to admit the application was wrong. She did not do so readily, and in the end, Tenuto seemed confused by her evasions. When Tenuto asked her what her real age was when she was Balnick's patient, Lorraine replied, "That has nothing to do with this case." She made this response to many of Tenuto's questions, and did the same when O'Neill asked her about Lenny's mental illnesses.

Bill finally got her to admit she had made the application out and the age on it was wrong. Possibly, Tenuto wanted the jury to believe Balnick treated Lorraine under the misapprehension she was under thirty-five. Or he may have wanted to point out to the jury we lived together before we were married, as Bill suggested. Either way, what he did made no sense. Bill and Steve had a good laugh about Tenuto's "grand strategy" to help his client escape liability.

O'Neill persisted in trying to make points with the old argument of Lorraine's brother Lenny's series of nervous breakdowns. Lorraine repeated several times that Lenny's problems were not part of Heather's problems. O'Neill also brought up one of my older sisters, Barbara, whose son, Eddy, had died in an institution of kernicterus. Neither of these conditions could have affected Heather, or would explain her condition, but O'Neill and Tenuto would return to them again and again. O'Neill could not explain what kernicterus was when he asked the question, and he asked it of Lorraine, not of me, initially. Since he could not tell us what it was, and since he was not a medical expert in any case, we had to wait until our final medical expert, Dr. Fisk, could explain what it was.

Fisk was one of the many neurologists we had consulted previously. He explained how he came to examine Heather, using three reports he had prepared, to the jury. Heather's visits were as a private outpatient. She had not been seen "on the wards," and the visits were part of our efforts to get help for the child. They were not originally consultations about a possible lawsuit.

From his first report Fisk read, "She was born after a very difficult labor lasting twenty-seven hours. Toward the end of the delivery, the heart rate slowed dangerously, and an emergency Caesarian section had to be performed." O'Neill would later make the point that the heart rate was not documented in the hospital records. Fisk said he got the information from us, or more likely, from Dr. Stein, who had access to the hospital records before Balnick had a chance to "correct" them. Fisk said he had not seen the hospital's records when he first saw Heather.

Fisk could not have gotten that information from us. We did not know about the irregular heart rate until the trial. The hospital records were on Fisk's desk the first time we took Heather to see him. I clearly remember seeing them. The notation about the irregular heartbeat is also in the University Hospital records. After the trial was over, all of the records used by Bill and his firm were given to me. I have seen the notation. The University Hospital staff got it from somewhere, at a time when details were fresh in people's minds. This notation must have been in the birth hospital's records.

Kernicterus could not explain Heather's condition, Fisk told the jury. Kernicterus is a "neurological condition, a condition of brain injury. It comes about when newborn babies are born RH positive from an RH negative mother who has been previously sensitized. This means a mother who is RH negative—negative means no antibodies—has a baby who is RH positive, with antibodies."

The only logical, consistent explanation of Heather's condition was "hypoxia," which occurred before and immediately after the birth. Emotional problems in other members of the family do not lead to profoundly retarded children. Kernicterus never happens with a first baby, which, of course, Heather was. The hospital had done a simple test when Lorraine was admitted which proves the RH factor in Lorraine's blood was no threat to Heather.

Concerning Heather's head circumference, Fisk said the size of her head was 34.5 cm. This is a normal size for a six-pound, five-ounce infant. She became microcephalic after birth. Her head never grew normally.

Fisk believed Heather might live to be thirty-five if she were maintained at home, "a little less if she were maintained in an institution." Bill had wanted Fisk to say forty years was a reasonable life expectancy for Heather, which Fisk felt he could not say. He did, however, add, "I cannot guess for Heather, as I cannot guess for anyone else in the room. The answer I give makes the assumption of nothing suddenly or untoward happening and also makes the assumption that I could be off by ten or fifteen years either way."

Bill was satisfied that Dr. Fisk had made another important part of our case and turned the questioning over to his adversaries.

> O'NEILL: Dr. Fisk, is it not true that an elderly prima gravida, such as Mrs. Zarecor was, has babies born with abnormalities in greater numbers than other women?
>
> FISK: They do. But the abnormality noted in babies born to older women is mongoloidism. Heather is clearly not mongoloid. Those statistical chances are not reflected in this case.
>
> TENUTO: Dr. Fisk, would you discuss Heather's self-awareness?
>
> FISK: That's a hard question to answer. She smiles, so presumably something happens that makes her. She doesn't smile at nothing. She smiles at something that makes her happy. And so she has an internal awareness. Internal awareness is difficult. She has feeling, if you will, because she smiles and cries.
>
> TENUTO: Yes, but Doctor, you've seen children more damaged than Heather, have you not?
>
> FISK: I would put it that most are damaged less.
>
> TENUTO: Well, then, those children "less damaged" than Heather, do they have a greater awareness of themselves as persons, as people able to have some relationship to the world outside of themselves, compared to Heather?
>
> FISK: I believe very strongly, as a matter of fact, that one's feelings or awareness are not directly proportionate to one's intelligence

or brightness or whatever one wants to say. We define "normal" in a certain way, but some children with an IQ of, for example, seventy-five, who fall outside the limits of "normal" have every bit the same kind of feelings we do. Part of the work I do is to spread the word.

TENUTO: What kind of IQ does Heather have?

FISK: I would have to say—I didn't check it—it would approach zero. I don't know.

JUDGE: Are you saying every human heart is human?

FISK: Yes, sir.

TENUTO: But there are degrees of sensitivity in human beings, are there not?

FISK: You can look at some of the smartest people in the United States or over the world, and they can still be among the most insensitive. You can look at some of the lower echelons in terms of intelligence, and they are the most caring, careful, and sensitive.

JUDGE: Thank you for your lecture on human sensibility.

Dr. Fisk was excused and left the stand. Bill told the court we would rest our case, but before leaving for the day, he wanted the court and other attorneys to witness something. A photographer Bill had hired came into the courtroom and took infrared pictures of various pages in the hospital record that Balnick had "corrected." Bill wanted to be able to show all the defense witnesses what was under Balnick's cross-outs.

O'Neill and Tenuto made one more pro forma motion to have the case dismissed on the grounds that we had not proven any negligence. Judge James denied their motions. O'Neill smiled and said he had not, in fact, expected any other ruling. The judge told O'Neill to start presenting the hospital's case on the next morning at 9:30 AM. Please be on time and ready to go, he said.

TWENY-NINE

O'Neill and Tenuto called eight witnesses between them. Not one of these witnesses would, or could, defend Balnick's conduct. A few even supported our contention about the cephalopelvic disproportion, or "CPD" as it was marked in the hospital's records. Another had a minor quibble about the term, but agreed the notation was "substantially correct." I wondered if this doctor would tell a patient she was "a little bit pregnant"? Either you are pregnant, or you aren't; either the birth difficulty was a cephalopelvic disproportion, or it wasn't, as far as I understood the issue.

Our case against the hospital was more openly challenged. O'Neill's first witness said their failure to take a urine sample on admission was a "departure from good and expected medical practice." But he disagreed with Dr. Kane about the consequences of this failure, and said it did not contribute to Heather's condition.

Several of the defense's witnesses tried to excuse Balnick's "correcting" the record, explaining, variously, that changes are made for reasons other than to hide facts. However, Bill got all of them to back off. Each admitted that Balnick's changes were not just "harmless" alterations of the record.

In the third week of the trial, two jurors had to drop out because of family issues and a third, a young woman, overslept and caused a two-hour delay in the start of a morning session. Judge James dismissed her immediately. By the last week of the trial, there were no alternate jurors left, and Bill became concerned one more juror would have to drop out, meaning the entire trial would have to start at the beginning again. When told of this possibility,

Lorraine said she was not certain she had the strength to go through this process one more time.

The shouting and carrying on between the attorneys and the witnesses became intolerable to me. I knew O'Neill and Tenuto had to present their cases, but what annoyed me was Bill's attitude. He seemed to consider each utterance by a defense witness a personal affront. He would turn red in the face, stand, and start shouting. This, to me, was a waste of time.

Obviously, Bill had to challenge the other side's statements, and he did so brilliantly, even though I say so as an extremely biased spectator. Still, while he was doing it, I could not help but wonder if there wasn't some shorter, more effective way. More than once, I thought I should simply tell Bill to shut up for a while, and let the trial get over. I did not, because, as Judge James had said earlier, nobody should interfere with an attorney trying a case.

My patience with the whole process was most severely tested when Bill cross-examined Dr. Leon Chartes, whom Tenuto had touted as his "star" expert witness. Chartes certainly had marvelous credentials: he was a member of the American Academy of Pediatrics, Section on Pediatric Neurology; he had affiliations with several hospitals; and he had official positions with foundations and state agencies. Chartes told Tenuto that during the twenty-two years he had practiced pediatric neurology, he had seen "children with brain damage and neurological problems numbering in the tens of thousands."

Chartes had examined Heather for the law firm representing Balnick on August 15, 1974 at a Manhattan hospital. Mark Billings accompanied Lorraine and Heather to the appointment. Heather was, at that time, about five-and-a-half years old.

Chartes was asked about his findings and replied, "She was an extremely disabled and limited child. She functioned on a profoundly infantile level. The terms 'idiot' and 'moron' were once used to describe Heather's level of intelligence."

A murmur went through the room. Judge James looked appalled at Chartes's use of those two terms. They were, Chartes conceded, unattractive and have long ago been discarded in the medical and mental health communities. Bill moved to have them struck and the judge instructed the jury to disregard them.

While Bill was cross-examining Chartes, he paused a lot. Sometimes the pause was a few seconds; sometimes it was a few minutes. Chartes would occasionally ask Bill why he was taking so long to ask questions. "Are you nervous, counselor?" Chartes would taunt.

The taunting came to a temporary stop after Bill responded, "I am just making certain I frame the question in such a way that you can't obfuscate and dodge an honest answer." Even I considered this to be excessive, and it brought protests from Tenuto and O'Neill. Judge James himself came down hard on Bill, admonishing him to treat the witness with the respect he, and the court, deserved.

I certainly did not believe Chartes deserved any respect and it occurred to me that perhaps Bill had to pause to prevent himself from saying what was truly on his mind, which was probably something in the order of, "Dr. Chartes, you weasel-son-of-a—" or other, worse curses.

In answering one question, Chartes told Bill he did not believe Heather had any self-awareness. Judge James seemed surprised at this statement.

> JUDGE: I beg your pardon—
>
> CHARTES (speaking rapidly): Heather can experience pain, but I don't think she sees herself as being abnormal compared to other people. If her IQ is zero or five, the ability to cerebrate and conceptualize is nothing. It doesn't exist.
>
> TENUTO: In your opinion, is Heather aware of her parents' "anguish" about her?
>
> CHARTES: I think she is totally unaware of that.
>
> TENUTO: What would you judge to be her life expectancy?
>
> CHARTES: It is unreasonable to expect Heather to live past the age of twenty-five years, give or take some years. It could be less, it could be more.
>
> TENUTO: And why is this?
>
> CHARTES: Heather cannot communicate. That exposes her to dangers of illnesses such as an ulcer or appendicitis. Heather's immobility predisposes her to lung infections, particularly what is called static or positional pneumonia. Heather's nutrition is poor ...

Lorraine let out an angry hiss. "It is not," she whispered to me. "The baby eats very well."

Chartes continued his long list of possible problems for Heather.

CHARTES: "Immobility leads to demineralization of bones, which cause, in turn, calcium stones in various organs of the body, especially in her kidneys. If she vomits, she could drown in her own regurgitated material. She is prone to infections. She cannot cough to clear her lungs. She could choke on food that went down the wrong tube. The phenobarbital prescribed to control her 'serious seizures' will weaken her resistance and expose her to greater dangers. She has developed a curvature of the spine, or scoliosis. Scoliosis might be treated by a surgical procedure, but Heather could not possibly survive that. The uncorrected scoliosis squeezes and compresses the heart and lungs. It compromises the ability of the lungs to ventilate as bellows and the heart to serve as a pump. It has a serious effect upon health and life expectancy. Finally, children like Heather are prone to sudden death. They can die in their sleep, and, in my experience, often do."

Tenuto, unbelievably, smiled broadly at his witness. He was acting as though he had just heard the best news he could possibly get.

TENUTO: Thank you. In your opinion, Doctor, is there any chance for this child to reach the age of, say, forty?

CHARTES: Not reasonable. But anything is possible.

A brief recess was then called. Bill told us in the hallway not be upset about what we'd just heard, because he was "going to destroy this guy twenty different ways."

In truth, I was not upset with Chartes's testimony. He had said nothing I didn't already know. Lorraine was biting her lip and seemed about to cry. Both of us managed to remain calm. Our real difficulty was not with the testimony, but with the trial itself, which was already near the end of its third week and seemed to have no end in sight.

When Chartes came into the hall, Bill waved a transcript from another trial in Chartes's direction. "I want to see him squirm out of this," he said loudly. "What do you think I should do with it, Ken?"

Bill made a grand gesture of showing me what was to me a virtually meaningless title page from the transcript. All I really understood about it was the date on the page, which was 1978. My first inclination was to suggest Bill use it as a weapon to slap Chartes around, but after one more second of reflection, I realized how close the whole trial was to chaos. The attorneys had resorted to some outrageous games, and the true meaning of why we were there seemed to be of no importance whatsoever.

Chartes and Bill had met in a courtroom several years before. The doctor had testified against one of Bill's clients, which was bad enough in Bill's eyes, but Chartes was a regular expert witness for insurance companies defending doctors being sued by patients. Since starting practice, Chartes had testified in approximately 125 cases. The vast majority of his testimony was given for insurance companies. Revenge can be sweet, I thought, but why does Bill have to use this trial to get it?

The transcript Bill kept waving at Chartes concerned a trial in which Chartes gave testimony on behalf of a claimant who was a patient of his. Bill and Chartes played a long, unpleasant game baiting each other about that trial. Everybody gave several shouts during the long struggle. By this time we had certainly heard enough shouting to be accustomed to it, but the longer the shouting went on, the louder it seemed to become. The egos of the attorneys and the doctors called to testify now seemed to be the main point of the trial. I was sick of it, and so, I think, was the judge, but it went on for several hours.

After Bill had asked Chartes for the third or fourth time to identify the trial transcript he was holding, Chartes got very loud.

> CHARTES: I cannot identify the trial! Tell me the parties involved.

> BILL: Perhaps you cannot remember the trial because you testify so much for insurance companies!

Tenuto, who had been on his feet most of the time, shouted about the unfairness of this line of questioning. It was unfair to the witness and would establish no facts concerning the present case, he said. Judge James, the only person who retained my respect during this phase of the trial, said he could not and would not attempt to interfere with any attorney's handling of a witness.

When Chartes finally did identify the case, Bill asked if Chartes's patient was not similar to Heather.

CHARTES: No, the cases are not similar. For one thing, this patient was mobile.

Bill had gone a long, tortuous route to make a single point: Chartes would testify for whomever would pay him. Chartes seemed unfazed when Bill had made that point.

Under further questioning he stated that the hospital record could not explain the cause of Heather's retardation. The deviations from accepted medical practice that the record indicated were also not an adequate explanation, he said. The taunting between Chartes and Bill resumed. "You are so nervous," Chartes said to Bill on one occasion, as Bill fumbled with his notes. He also said several times, "You are so uptight."

Bill's movements betrayed anger and frustration, but he did not respond. I am certain he kept quiet because of Judge James's earlier admonition. Once, after an especially trying series of questions and evasions, Bill shook his head sadly and looked up to the ceiling before repeating a question. Chartes smirked and demanded, "Who are you asking, me or God?"

Chartes continued to insist that nothing could explain Heather's retardation except some factor no one could know at the time of the birth, or now, for that matter. Judge James disallowed such suggestions, saying they could be used by the jury to reach a verdict only if the statements were medical knowledge as known and practiced in 1969.

In the end, all the shouting and drama were useless and meaningless. Chartes destroyed his own credibility better than even Bill could have dreamed was possible.

Chartes, in spite of the judge's rulings disallowing such statements, made another statement that Heather's problems were the result of an unknown and mysterious cause, not the work of the hospital or Balnick.

BILL: How can you continue to make these statements? Have you reviewed the hospital record? The events leading up to Heather's birth, the events after her birth, the resuscitative procedures, and so forth?

CHARTES: No.

Chartes showered Bill with a manic smile, but Bill did not see it. He was looking at his notes to frame the next question. The tension in the courtroom became more pronounced as Bill continued to study his notes. Suddenly, Bill looked up and did a double take. Steve half rose in his chair and put a hand on Bill's arm. Bill looked and sounded as though he did not believe what he had just heard.

BILL: You have not?

CHARTES: No.

BILL: Do I understand that your opinion, with respect to causal connection that you have, does not include a review of the hospital record?

CHARTES: That's correct.

Chartes continued smiling broadly at Bill and looked in turn at Tenuto (who had put a hand to his head) and the judge. Judge James did not return the smile. He was glaring at Chartes. "Do I understand you never looked at the hospital record?"

Bill did not want the moment destroyed, even if for the best of intentions. "I think that is what he said, Your Honor. I don't want to ask him any more questions about it."

Judge James was not deterred, and turned his angry look toward Bill.

JUDGE: I want to make it clear.

CHARTES: That's what I said.

Chartes nodded and looked very pleased with himself. He actually looked as though he were about to burst out in laughter or song.

Bill also looked very pleased, and did have a smile in his voice when he said, "I have no further questions."

There was a long silence in the courtroom. Tenuto said nothing. He still had a hand to his head, massaging his forehead. After he massaged his forehead, he massaged the back of his neck.

Finally, Judge James asked, "Mr. Tenuto?"

Tenuto stopped massaging for a moment. "No further questions."

Judge James excused Chartes, but did not add the customary "Thank you for your testimony." O'Neill thanked the doctor as he rushed out of the courtroom. Tenuto, who had called Chartes to be a witness, said nothing and did not look in his direction as the doctor left. I thought it was a wonderful, well-deserved ending to Chartes. All of Bill's well-planned ambush of this man he clearly considered an enemy turned out to be a waste of time. I know many attorneys came into the courtroom to witness Bill in action, and I know Chartes's behavior was much discussed among them. I have often wondered if Chartes was ever hired to be an expert witness again. It is my sincere hope that his expert testimony days ended that day, once and for all.

Tenuto produced two more witnesses, both excellent and well-meaning men. Neither offered much comfort to Balnick. One may have damaged the hospital's case.

The first said the obstetrical care given by Balnick was "lousy." He also tried to advance theories to explain away the causes of Heather's retardation. The extent of the "damage" simply could not be explained by even the unprofessional and "bad" care given to Lorraine. Judge James refused to allow most of this doctor's testimony.

This doctor tried to lay blame at the hospital's door by emphasizing the fact that the doctors treating Lorraine were all first- and second-year interns. They were simply not qualified to deal with the kinds of problems encountered "in this delivery." He added they were probably afraid to approach Balnick, who might treat such "help" with anger or scorn.

The last of Tenuto's expert witnesses had examined Heather several times when we lived in Manhattan. He was associated with some of the early programs we took Heather to. He said, simply, he felt it was unrealistic to expect her to live to be forty years of age. I think he was brought in with the hope of recovering some of the ground lost by Chartes. Steve told me Tenuto was doing no more with his final witnesses than trying to buy a partner in the damages. Personally, I thought he was doing no more than attempting to delay the inevitable day of judgment.

One of Bill's colleagues to whom I talked a lot during the trial told me he felt the insurance companies were mostly at fault for our nine-year wait to get to trial. I did not entirely agree, but I was sure the insurance companies were certainly part of the blame. It still seems to me that our own law firm could have pursued them more aggressively. The insurance companies would use every possible tactic for delay, I was told, on the hope Heather would die. For them, it was a simple matter of dollars versus the child's life. Their interest was dollars. Ours was her life. I felt Tenuto and O'Neill were both stalling this trial, hoping against hope to find some way to save dollars.

When Tenuto finished his case, we offered one rebuttal witness. It was Steve. He was called to rebut more of the testimony Chartes had given.

Chartes claimed our estimates of the costs to keep Heather at home were too high. He even claimed he knew of several institutions that were ready to accept Heather immediately. Steve checked out each statement made by Chartes. My experience was verified. None of the institutions mentioned by Chartes would accept a child with Heather's "involvement," and several associations for the handicapped had agreed that $80,000 per year was a reasonable estimate of the cost of keeping Heather at home.

The trial was, at long last, nearing its end. Tenuto, O'Neill, and Bill, in that order, would do their summations. Judge James would then charge the jury and the case would be theirs.

THIRTY

While the trial was going on, I got a call—a couple of calls, actually—from Margaret Connor, the head teacher in Heather's classroom at United Cerebral Palsy in Brooklyn. On the first call, she said, "I'm calling to invite you to visit us. We have something to show you. I know you will be very pleased."

"Really?" I answered. At the time of Margaret's first call, I had just finished my first period giving testimony, and was on call to go back whenever Bill felt I should. I explained that to Margaret, and she told me to please get in touch with her when I could go to the school.

After no more than two days, she called again to see if I could go. The specific day she wanted me at the school, I was scheduled to testify. Finally, I had been excused from testifying, and I told her when she called I would be there the next day about lunchtime.

As I entered Heather's classroom, Margaret said, "I'm glad you're here. Heather is getting impatient waiting for her lunch."

Heather was seated in a chair at the table. Her right hand was placed on the table and held there by one of the teacher's aides. Margaret sat behind her, and began guiding the spoon into the food. Margaret sang, rather than spoke, to Heather as she guided the spoon from the food to Heather's mouth. Heather was hungry—she ate the food readily.

After guiding two or three bites into Heather's mouth, Margaret let go of the spoon, leaving it in Heather's hand. Heather beat the spoon on the plastic plate and lifted it to throw it, but Margaret guided it back to the food and gave Heather one more bite of food. She repeated the process of guiding the food one more time and then let go of Heather's hand again. Heather guided the spoon to the food and stuck it into the food. When she lifted the spoon to her mouth there was not much food on it, but she repeated the process one more time. After tasting the nearly empty spoon the second time, Heather started to wave it, getting ready to give it a toss. Margaret quickly intervened and helped Heather guide the spoon from the plate to her mouth two or three more times.

"Now, you should try it," Margaret said to me. I sat behind Heather and whispered into her ear. She leaned into my chest and smiled. Margaret laughed and said, "You know, her reaction to you is different from her reaction to Lorraine."

"Yeah," I said. "We have noticed that, too. She always smiles and laughs when she hears Lorraine's voice. When she senses I am around, she leans into me or holds out her left hand, as if wanting to be played with."

"That is what we have seen. What our staff psychologist finds so interesting about it is the fact that she will do those things for you two only—for nobody else. She definitely seems to know who her mommy and daddy are."

When I took Heather's hand and put the spoon in it, she handed the spoon back to me. I tried it again, but got the spoon back again. I then kept her hand in mine and guided it into the food and into her mouth. After feeding her several bites, I let go of the spoon. This time, Heather banged it on the plate a couple of times and then started to wave it in preparation for another toss.

"I think she is probably full," Margaret said, "but let's see how she holds the milk." She poured milk into a plastic glass and handed it to me.

"Here is some milk," I said to Heather. "Your favorite." There have always been periods when Heather refused to drink anything but milk. Heather eagerly took the glass and drank. I let go of it, and she continued to drink for a short time. Suddenly, she seemed to be aware she held the glass in her hand without assistance. The milk and the glass went flying through the air.

After the mess was cleaned up, Margaret explained to me the details of teaching Heather to feed herself. "Heather used to cry a lot when she came into the classroom. But since we have started this behavior modification program with her, that has stopped."

"A behavior modification program?" I asked.

"Yes. We wanted to try to get her to stop sucking her finger and to get rid of those plastic keys that she always has in her mouth when she comes into the classroom. The program goes like this: one of us in the class sits beside Heather and holds her hand for one minute. We let it go for one minute. If she doesn't put the finger or the keys back in her mouth, she is rewarded with a spoonful of applesauce. We keep this up for half an hour a day. The times for her not to return the finger or keys to her mouth keep getting longer—yesterday Heather was successful for a period of ten minutes. A side reward that we had not expected was to calm her down. It seems that she was just crying for attention, or for missing her mommy and daddy."

"That is probably correct," I agreed. "I know she doesn't cry much at home anymore." For both of us, the fact that Heather rarely cried was a heaven-sent blessing. "She gets somebody's undivided attention all the time there. But tell me, how long did it take you to get her to feed herself?"

"It is optimistic of you to say she feeds herself. But she is getting closer and we are pleased with all the signs of progress. The process of training for the finger-sucking and the feeding are virtually the same, and as one improves, the other one improves, too. For us, also, the biggest gain is that Heather seems to be much calmer nearly all the time. She hasn't had a tantrum for months."

Before I left, I wrote a note to Heather's neurologist, saying that the school had my permission to discuss Heather's medication with him. The school had noted that the improvements were not sustained on a regular basis—some days she remembered the drill, some days she would have no part of it. Margaret thought that his input on the matter would be helpful.

On my next visit to Brooklyn, I seated myself behind Heather at the kitchen table and tried to get her to feed herself. Heather got only three or four bites of food this way, so I eventually ended up feeding her.

Lorraine was not altogether pleased. "Well," she said, "now I know why the kid comes home hungry most days. They are not really feeding her at that school. It is good to try to get her to do things for herself, but we can't starve the baby doing it."

UCP kept trying to train Heather, and I followed their plan when I was with her, but Lorraine did not, or did so half-heartedly. This program went on for another year, until Heather started having more severe seizures. Eventually the skill was lost after a hospitalization and was never recovered. Now she will hold the spoon, but will make no attempt to feed herself.

THIRTY-ONE

On December 5, 1979 Judge James asked the jury to listen to the attorneys' summations. "This is the only place," he told them, "when each attorney is entitled for the first time, the only time, to comment on the evidence."

Tenuto rose to speak for Balnick. "There is no question," he told the jury, "that Dr. Balnick should have attended Mrs. Zarecor in the hospital. We raise for you the question of whether that omission was a contributing or substantial factor contributing to Heather Zarecor's brain damage. Dr. Balnick was not in the hospital, but somebody was there. It wasn't a question of being unattended.

"Dr. Balnick was in constant communication with the hospital. It is up to you, the jury, to decide whether or not the communications were, in fact, correct communications. That is, if the proper information was given.

"The allegation of a cover-up is difficult. It would appear, from the fact that certain records are missing, that the cover-up was an essential part of this case. Dr. Balnick contends he does not remember what happened. That makes sense to me. It certainly makes a great deal of sense to me eight or ten years later, when the case comes to trial, to say, 'I don't remember anymore.'

"The causes of action against everyone, except Dr. Balnick and the hospital, have been dropped by the plaintiff. Two causes of action remain. The first reads, 'The plaintiff, Kenneth Zarecor, as the father of the infant plaintiff, claims medical and other expenses both past and future.'" We made no claim for past expenses, simply because we realized future expenses might approach $80,000 per year, in 1979 costs. Past medical expenses totaled $50,000 in out-of-pocket expenses. My insurance companies paid much more to cover the costs of doctor visits and hospital stays. Rather than cloud the issue over past expenses, however, we concentrated on what we knew would be the major costs—future expenses.

"It would be wrong to award money for past medical expenses," Tenuto continued. "No case has been made for any past medical expenses.

"The second remaining cause of action reads, 'The infant plaintiff, Heather Zarecor, sustained injuries to her person, including internal injuries, and was caused to suffer and will continue to suffer severe physical pain and mental anguish and that such injuries are of a permanent nature.'

"Now, you, the jury, will have to award a sum of money you feel appropriate, assuming the second cause of action is 'correct.' No claim is made for the parents for their pain, their suffering, their embarrassment, and their anguish. There is no claim for any damages, and you must not award damages to the parents. If you do, you are doing wrong. If you agree with the plaintiffs, you will award damages to Heather. In doing so, however, you should consider if you scarred Heather Zarecor's face, she would not know the difference. I mean it is an awful thing to say, but you have to face the facts. She has no awareness of herself.

"The final question," Tenuto said, "is 'How long is she going to live?' I don't think she is going to die five years from now, but she may die tomorrow. I do know this: her chances of going fifteen years on the other side of thirty-five are impossible, in my opinion, and I think the doctors have told you that."

As Tenuto spoke, I could feel Lorraine, sitting beside me, get more and more tense. I winced and, I am certain, ground my teeth as he spoke. Tenuto was working under some duress, himself. Not only was he straining to hear during the trial, it also turns out that he had suffered a tragedy in his family the week before the trial began—one of his brothers had caught a group of kids trying to steal his car, confronted them, and was shot to death. Still, after listening to him utter a series of gross and insensitive statements about handicapped people, and Heather in particular, I could only feel that he was in way over his head—he simply was not up to the task at hand.

O'Neill's closing statement for the jury was brief and, as usual, contained factual errors, two big ones coming right off the bat: "There is a history of mental or emotional disturbances in both the Zarecors' families," he began. Bill objected to this statement. There is no such history in my family, and while the defendants brought up Lorraine's brother, they made no attempt to establish anything about the cause of his breakdowns. Kernicterus, in case O'Neill did not know it, is not a mental illness. The judge said such statements, as would all parts of the attorneys' summations, would be covered in instructions to the jury.

In response to Bill's objections, O'Neill added, "They have tried to play it down." Again, Bill objected, stating that the defense would never have known anything about either of our families' medical histories from information they gathered. He got the information he used from the records of the doctors who examined Heather. In other words, we gave it to him, even if indirectly. If we had wanted to "play it down," we would never have discussed it when going to any doctor.

"The only case against the hospital is based on the word of Dr. Balnick. This was a man who was responsible for a horror. And he says, 'I don't remember.' On the witness stand, he says residents or interns or departments gave him wrong information. I submit to you that if the residents, or the X-ray department, told Dr. Balnick the wrong thing, it would be all over the record, and he wouldn't tell you 'I don't remember.' My point is that the only testimony against the hospital is based on the assumption Dr. Balnick was not properly told. The only person's word we have for that is a liar: a liar who is trying to push it over on the residents and the hospital because he did the wrong thing. He didn't show up. I ask you in this case to put the blame where it belongs. And Dr. Balnick is solely to blame, not the hospital."

Then O'Neill took his seat.

Both these summations assumed the jury verdict would be against their clients. O'Neill had been mercifully brief. He had been angry with Dr. Kane and upset with me, but in his summation, he expressed downright hostility to Balnick. Tenuto had been disturbing and ugly. He had implied that Heather was so severely damaged any award to her by the jury would be meaningless. Did Tenuto believe the jury would be easier on Balnick because Heather would never be able to fully appreciate their judgment?

After a lunch break, Bill Dugan rose and explained to the jury how we saw the case. "There are some forgotten people in this case," Bill began. "Heather, Lorraine, Ken, Dr. Balnick, and the hospital staff. You will decide the case considering the forgotten people, not the attorneys who have put on such a display arguing the case, nor Judge James, who tried it. Only you, the jury, can decide where the truth lies. It is for you, having done that, to then, without fear, without prejudice, without sympathy, to decide whether damages should be awarded on the two remaining causes of action.

"What we are about at this point is not compassion for Lorraine, for Ken, and not compassion for Heather. We are about money. It comes down to that. Crass, isn't it?

"This case is about a basic betrayal of trust. We live our lives on trust. You and I depend upon the trustworthiness of others. We deal with the auto mechanic. Trust. A television repairman. Trust. A lawyer. Trust. But, if any of these breach our trust, no one's brain is damaged.

"Lorraine went to Dr. Balnick, a man of skills, a specialist. She placed her trust in him. She did not go into the hospital with the idea of being treated by interns, or some first-year medical students. She had a right to expect her labor would be documented accurately and fairly. She had a right to believe that if there were some change in her condition, something would be done about it. She had a right to believe her doctor would be notified and that he would be there. She placed her trust in professionals—Dr. Balnick and all those doctors at the hospital.

"Lorraine is in the hospital. Ken calls Dr. Balnick. He gets the service. Ken calls several more times, never getting answers to his questions. 'Why are you panicking?' Dr. Balnick asks. 'They tell me she is doing nothing. Why do you panic?' Does Ken Zarecor know about ineffectual labor? Trust. Does Ken Zarecor know about an elderly prima gravida, who should be watched closely? Trust. What could the husband of the patient be expected to know about the X-ray or a cephalopelvic disproportion? Does Ken know about that? Trust.

"Whether or not Dr. Balnick was informed by the hospital, it doesn't relieve him of the responsibility to attend Lorraine, who put her trust in him. He should have been there. You know it. He knows it. We all know it. He abandoned her. For what reason? To this minute, you and I don't know.

"Our legal team took a risk having a new pelvimetry done. What did we know? What did we know the pelvimetry was going to show? The truth will never get you into trouble.

"Records were altered, records are missing. Judge James will tell you later that you have a right to infer that if those records came in, they would not be favorable to their defense. These records aren't in the control of Ken or Lorraine. They certainly are not in the control of Heather. Trust. Trust."

Bill paused and took a sip of water, looked at each of the jurors, and continued.

"Please recall Ken's testimony of a frantic call from Dr. Balnick: 'I am looking at the X-rays, your baby can't be born. We have to operate.' Does that have a ring of truth in it?"

Bill pointed to me, sitting beside Lorraine in the public section. "This man, back in '69, what does he know about X-rays? He gave that testimony four years ago, and he was the first to be examined at that examination before trial. What does he know about X-ray pelvimetry?

"What was the hospital doing? What were those residents and interns and chiefs of service doing? They were sitting on their hands.

"The panic, the guilt that must have gone through Balnick's mind. 'My God, why wasn't I there before?' Where was he? Where was he? Does he know where he was? Oh, come on—how many brain-damaged children did he bring into the world? God hopes only one. One is too many. One is her only one and his only one." Bill was pointing to both of us. "These people for whom this case is all about. Lorraine is on the stand, this hero who spent the last ten years—they don't want five cents for that ten years—because they accepted this child and they want this child and this child has brought a lot of love into their home.

"And did you hear them when it came to damages?" Bill waved in the direction of Tenuto and O'Neill. "Do you hear them? The insensitivity of this. 'Because we didn't show for twenty-four hours,' this is Balnick, through his lawyer, 'and this baby was really deprived of oxygen, we so brain-damaged her that if she had a scar on her face, she wouldn't be sensitive to it.' Oh, my God! What an argument! How indelicate can you be? How far do we go in order to try to wipe out any form of dignity in Heather Zarecor?

"Our expert and experts for the defense confirmed cephalopelvic disproportion. Even Balnick, this man who didn't come back on the stand as part of Tenuto's defense, confirmed it.

"Our claim against the hospital does not rest on whether or not you believe Balnick when he tells you he wasn't informed. Balnick can be believed on this part of his testimony. He would be a beast if the contrary were true. But Balnick did not come, whether or not he was told. And the hospital did nothing. One witness for the defense had said there should have been feverish activity."

Bill looked to be near exhaustion, and the most difficult part of his summation was still before him.

"I know you will reach the point of awarding damages," he went on. "If that is presumption, so be it. Do not cheat Heather. We do not know how medical science will do it, but her chances of living a long life improve every day. Do not shortchange Heather. When you determine future expenses it would be better to err on the side of an increased life expectancy than leave her wanting in the future. Once she has a verdict in court, that's it. If she reaches forty, she can't come back and say, 'Jurors, I'm still here.'

"A famous trial lawyer used to talk to jurors, when he came to damages, of the interference with the enjoyment of life. Heather's life has already been interfered with. Is Heather able to see? Is Heather able to walk? To stand? To romp? She is past that. She was one, she was two, she was seven, and she is ten. Did she play with a teddy bear? Did she play with dolls? Did she read the comics? Have a bike? How about the park? The pool? The friendship of others? Dress up in Mommy's clothes? She is a little lady. What is her future? Dance? Skate? Marry? Fall in love? Enjoy the beauty of a sunset? The joy of her parents? Change of seasons? Can you put a figure on those deprivations?"

A long silence followed. Bill, Lorraine, and I composed ourselves. Judge James, who was also obviously moved by Bill's final words, cleared his throat before he spoke. "Ladies and gentlemen," he said, "this will be all this afternoon. I want to emphasize that you must not discuss the case with anyone or among yourselves. Tomorrow morning, I will charge the jury. Then the case will be yours."

My impatience and annoyance with Bill had evaporated. If I say so myself, his summation was superb. It laid before the jury all the facts. It showed clearly the consequences of Balnick's and the hospital's failures. His words were compelling, touching, and honest. We had waited nine interminable years to have our day in court. Bill gave as good a summation of our case as we could have hoped for.

THIRTY-TWO

The next day brought another of the shocks that seemed to attend this case. The cause of action on behalf of me as Heather's father for "future medical and other expenses" was incorrectly drawn by the absent and unlamented Mark Billings. Under state law, such awards could only be made to Heather.

"Mark Billings wrote the original complaint," I snapped to Steve, as he tried to apologize away Mark's error. "This is one more proof that whatever he did, he did under the pressure of a deadline, such as filing the complaint the day before the statute of limitations expired. He was always working in a sort of hurry-up, near-panic mode. Mark's been gone two or three years now, but he is still gumming up the works."

"He's a good attorney," Steve told me. "He did a brilliant examination before trial."

For O'Neill and Tenuto, this was the first good news they had had in weeks. They moved to have the second cause of action dismissed. They also moved to have a mistrial declared because Bill had been emotional in his summation. "He used the word 'God' no less than twenty-seven times," O'Neill said, while Tenuto complained angrily and bitterly of being held up to ridicule and abuse by Bill.

Judge James reserved decision on their motions, but he did say he would charge the jury in such a way that future medical expenses must be included in the verdict "for the infant." As the complaint stood, "the parents are entitled to nothing." He continued, "I will not unsuit this child if liability is made out against the hospital and Dr. Balnick. I will not unsuit this child in regard to what is already apparent, namely she will require careful, expensive medical treatment for the rest of her life. That is all I am going to do. I will recoil violently from any other idea."

Bill joked with me later that he would call his insurance company to get ready for a "huge suit" if our case was ever thrown out of court because of this error. I failed to see any humor in the situation. In fact, to this very day, I am not all that amused by this turn of events.

Judge James gave his charge to the jury on Thursday morning. They deliberated until Friday afternoon, December 7, 1979. Lorraine got very impatient with the wait for a verdict, but I did not. The jury sent three notes, each one asking to see another piece of evidence. When they asked to see the X-ray and X-ray report taken at Dr. Kane's office, I did wonder how they were going to be able to read it, and if anyone on the jury had some kind of medical expertise, but I also thought their requests showed the jury was taking the task of examining the evidence presented seriously. That, in my opinion, could only benefit us.

As we were waiting on a verdict on Friday morning, Lorraine said she could stand the suspense no longer and went home. If she had waited only a few hours longer, she would have heard the jury award Heather one million dollars for pain and suffering, and $933,000 for future medical expenses. The foreman of the jury told us the latter figure was arrived at by multiplying the number of years they thought she would survive by the amount they determined would be needed to care for her. The verdict was against the hospital and Balnick, and it was unanimous, save for one juror who felt Balnick should be held solely liable.

Before Judge James could dismiss the jury, they had to "state the percentage of fault attributable to each defendant and the total amount of these percentages must equal one hundred." This deliberation took less than fifteen minutes. The jury found the liability was "ninety percent for Dr. Balnick, and ten percent for the hospital."

Judge James thanked the jury for their work, as did Bill and the other attorneys. When the jury was dismissed, Bill, Steve, Tenuto, and I went to talk to them. The foreman told me all the jurors were strongly impressed with Lorraine and me. "We all felt you were honest, brave people," he told me.

The juror who did not want the hospital held liable apologized to me after Steve explained to her why it was important that the hospital be held responsible, along with Balnick. He said, simply, that if both defendants were held liable, we stood a better chance of collecting the entire judgment. As Bill had said in his summation, Steve made it sound as though it all came down to money, in the end. I told the lady she need not apologize, especially since her opinion did not prevail. Before she left, she told me she felt better knowing people like Lorraine and me were "still around." She asked God's blessing on Heather and us, and gave me a prayer card that gave thanks for all of God's goodness.

Bill asked the jury members if they believed our cephalopelvic disproportion contention. They did, one juror told him, based on the evidence presented and on the fact that they opened pages of the hospital record that had been stapled shut. Inside those stapled pages they found "CPD" notations. Those notations had not been crossed out or tampered with.

When I thanked one of the jurors, she said, "You don't have to thank us, and you really should not thank us. I, for one, am proud that I was part of this. It was a fascinating trial and it ended properly. The good guys won this one. I think we did a good and moral thing today. Everyone on the jury agreed. We redressed a wrong that needed redressing."

After talking to the jurors, I went to Brooklyn to see Lorraine and Heather, as I had done every Friday since I left their household. Lorraine was not sure what the verdict meant. Bill had explained to her about the possibility of appeals and the fact that insurance companies would not pay a large verdict without fighting. The fight could last several years, he told her. "So we won, and that's great," Lorraine said, "but how many years will we wait before the victory comes home?"

I called Fanny and explained the verdict to her. "Thank God," she said. "Maybe now you and Lorraine can do something for yourselves." In her customary upbeat and optimistic way, she also added that she hoped we would collect the judgment "before you are in your graves."

A few weeks after the judgment, Bill called me. It was the first of a series of long conversations about a compromise settlement or letting the case go to appeal. Bill argued strongly for letting the case go to appeal. He believed the case was so strong the Appellate Division of the New York State Supreme Court would uphold all or most of the verdict. We might get the largest amount ever in such a case in New York State, he said. Clearly, setting that record was a cherished goal of his. It was not a goal we cherished, or even considered worth pursuing, because the process would take several years, at a minimum.

Bill was encouraged in his belief that most of the verdict would be upheld when Tenuto told him Balnick's insurance company would settle in the amount of $975,000. Bill laughed when he told me they wanted to save only $25,000 of his million-dollar policy. O'Neill offered $200,000 as the hospital's share of the compromise agreement. He told me the hospital's carrier could and would do better.

Lorraine and I, however, were close to exhaustion from the tensions of the trial and by problems of caring for Heather. We felt we could not tolerate the thought of waiting for a long appeals process. The realization that the Appellate Division could decide, in their wisdom, to send the case back for retrial did not make us feel any better.

I told Bill about a conversation that I had overheard between O'Neill and Tenuto, while we were waiting for the verdict. They were discussing the grounds for an appeal of any verdict that came in. It did, of course, occur to me that the discussion was for my benefit, since they knew I was in the courtroom awaiting the verdict, as they were. They said Judge James should not have allowed me to testify as I did, and he should not have allowed Steve to testify at all. There were three or four other "errors" that could be used in an appeal, they said.

As the summations came to a close, more and more attorneys came into Judge James's courtroom to see the action. I talked to several of them as the trial progressed. It turned out some of them had watched me testify. Bill had told them to. "This man will, by himself," Bill had told one of the attorneys, "nail Balnick's coffin shut. Our experts will put him in the coffin, but Ken will nail it shut for us." When I talked to them about the defense's threats to appeal the case, all of them told me it was unlikely they would have any luck. Our case, I was told, was airtight. The Appellate Division would just cut the verdict, and maybe not even do that. What they did not say, however, was that the appellate process could take years.

These attorneys thought there was almost no chance the case would be returned for retrial. They said it was not impossible, but not likely. As in everything else, nobody could guarantee anything, of course. Judge James had made mistakes and all the mistakes seemed to be in our favor, but they were, to be certain, minor errors. It had been all any attorney or client could hope for: a fair trial. The Appellate Division might think the cumulative effect of the errors, however, while not doing damage to Balnick's defense, did harm the case of the hospital.

Lorraine told me to do what I thought best, "Especially since you make the decisions, anyway." Then she added, "Tell Bill to settle the case." That is what I did. We did not, in truth, consider anything else for more than ten minutes. Bill said, again, that his advice was that we wait. We can get a million-five, not just a million-two. "No," I told Bill, "Settle. A million-two in 1980 is as good as a million-five will be in 1983 or 1985, or whenever the appeals are done. And neither Lorraine nor I can stand the thought of going through another trial."

Bill assured me there was virtually no possibility of another trial, but we still did not want to go through the appeal process. "Then give us 120 days to settle the case for you," Bill pleaded. I gave him sixty days and told him to do the best he could. After further negotiations, the hospital's carrier did raise their settlement offer to $350,000. The total amount of the compromise settlement was $1,325,000.

Judge James looked around for ways of letting us have access to the money for Heather's use without going through a lot of constant red tape dealing with another court, namely the Surrogate's Court. In the end, however, he could not make things easy for us under New York State law. The Kings County Surrogate's Court is our silent partner in caring for Heather. We report to the court once a year on what was spent and how the money is invested.

Dugan and Tuscano's fee was $333,763.06. Judge James cut the six cents off. They also got $16,948 for expenses incurred. We were given $20,000 for "immediate assistance" in setting up a suitable residence for Heather. The balance of the money was initially put into nineteen savings accounts in eighteen banks. At that time, during the years of the Carter inflation, the banks were paying twelve and fourteen percent interest, so we didn't lose that much.

Since the initial deposits, the Surrogate's Court has given us permission to invest as "we" see fit. The "we," in this case, should read "I." This was the source of many long and bitter arguments between Lorraine and me. She— and Fanny, who seemed to be the real source of Lorraine's concerns—never seemed to understand any investment vehicle other than a savings account. When I invested the money in a house, or in stocks, bonds, or mutual funds,

Lorraine thought the money had disappeared, and had disappeared into my pockets. She actually asked me, "How are you getting this money? You may know where it is, but how do I know it will be there when I need it?" I did take some time to show her the asset and bank accounts, which she seemed to understand, but I would be asked the same questions later.

In all the years I have watched over the investment of Heather's money, the single comment made by Lorraine, other than to wonder why I just didn't leave it in savings accounts, was to complain once when I showed her a list of the stocks Heather owned. That list included a tobacco company. "No, no," Lorraine said, "we can't be involved with a company like that." That stock was sold.

The income from the investments has never paid the full amount of the costs of Heather's care. Because I invested in houses, and the houses appreciated in value and were sold at the appreciated value, the amount of the original insurance payment is intact. The market value of the bonds we now hold is lower than the investment value, but I have confidence that all of our capital will be returned to us. My strategy for investing Heather's money has been conservative—I wish I had been that careful and wise in investing my own money, but that is all water under the bridge, as they say.

THIRTY-THREE

There are, of course, more parts to this story.

In the years after the court case, I went to Brooklyn College and got a bachelor's and a master's degree in American history. I went into teaching and, after a rough start, ended up teaching Special Education in a hospital program in Far Rockaway, New York. Lorraine said it was because I was Special Ed myself, but Special Ed kids and I seemed to be an excellent fit. I had disliked teaching high school and found teaching an elementary school class of thirty-five very difficult. For some reason, I could handle any group of even the most needy and problematic twelve or fourteen kids.

Lorraine did some traveling, but her health declined at a pretty constant pace. Finally, in December 2001, due to renal failure, Lorraine's body retained a huge amount of water. She became virtually helpless, and one Sunday night she did not call me as usual to help her to the bathroom, and she fell. She had fallen before, and I had been able to help her up without much trouble. On this night, with the added weight from the water retention, I could not lift her, and we had to make a 911 medical emergency call. The two attendants, taking one look at Lorraine, suggested she go immediately to the hospital, and we agreed.

When I called her doctor, a bird-like woman named Bauman, to inform her of the hospitalization, the doctor told me that Lorraine was her most "noncompliant" patient. For years, I had ferried Lorraine around to various doctors and she had treated them all with disdain, to say the least. She would often tell me all the doctors were doing her no good and quoted the line of Alexander the Great: "I am dying with the help of too many doctors." When

I would point out that she could not expect good results unless she followed their orders, she would reply, "Doctors are not nearly as smart as they think they are."

Bauman asked me if I knew Lorraine had just been diagnosed with multiple myeloma. I reminded her she had called me to tell me. "Things aren't good, Mr. Zarecor, but she probably has some life left. Of course, if the cancer doesn't kill her, I might."

At this time, I was teaching in a hospital program in Queens for emotionally disturbed children. I was also the chapter leader for the United Federation of Teachers and, fortunately, had a union function to attend and did not have to go to my school at my usual time of 7:30 AM. I took the opportunity to go to the hospital to see Lorraine before going to my meeting. When I went into her room, she was sitting on the bed, reading the *New York Times.*

"There is no good news, again," Lorraine said. "I just thank God that trailer trash Bill and the evil witch Hillary are no longer around, embarrassing us." In another of her political obsessions, Lorraine came to despise both Hillary and Bill Clinton and anyone associated with them. In bad times, she would sit in front of the television and curse at any member of the Clinton administration that came on the screen. I did not really care that Lorraine had turned from being a classic New York liberal into a person who embraced Republican conservatism, but her idolization of Sean Hannity and Rush Limbaugh was more than I could handle. We made an agreement that she would listen to them in her bedroom with the door closed if I was in the house.

After making some small talk about the house and Heather's program, I told Lorraine I needed to catch a train into Manhattan to go the union meeting. "You and your school and now the union," Lorraine said, rolling her eyes. "I am glad you found something to occupy yourself with. Maybe you give them too much time?"

"Let's discuss that when you get home," I said, and stood to leave.

"Wait a second," Lorraine said. "I think we need to talk about something."

She paused as I stood and looked at her. She returned my look and then looked away before resuming. "I think I am dying. I don't think I will ever get back home."

"Dr. Bauman told me she thought you had some time left," I said.

"She's hoping so, so she can torture me," Lorraine said. We both laughed, and Lorraine continued. "No, you surely see for yourself that I look like hell revisited. Everyone says you speak truth in a simple, direct way. I'm surprised you haven't said something—"

"I'm not sure telling someone they look sick would be a kind or necessary conversation. I guess that would be what your mother called a 'Jewish compliment.' And you are immune to following doctor's directions, anyway."

Lorraine raised her hand. "Yeah, I know. That's an old conversation. But, whatever the fact is, we should talk. You know you never talked that much, even before you left, and not since you came back, either."

I sat back down. "That is also a conversation we have had many times before. It can't be solved here. What is it that you want to say?"

"First, I guess I have to say that I am sorry about a few things."

"You sure you want to do this now? Maybe when you are feeling better, stronger, we can talk about rights and wrongs—"

"No, no. First, I am almost certain I won't be coming home again." I started to protest that there was no way she could know that but instead let her continue. "I feel like I can't go on. I have more pain each day, and I am just not sure I can go on—" Lorraine paused, and sighed deeply. "But I don't want to cry, so let's do this talk."

"Have you asked the doctors for painkillers? That you would take?" I asked.

"No, that isn't the issue. It is clear to me my time has run out, and I don't want to sleep through it, painful as it is."

Another silence followed. Lorraine finally began again. "I am sorry that I put you through so much *tragedya*. I suppose you should have known from the start about Pa's mental illness—" Lorraine referred to the fact that, contrary to what I had been told, Lorraine's dad died in a mental institution. "But Ma always said if you knew you would be out the door like a shot, and you would take Heatherel with you."

"If I had known, I probably would have tried even harder to get you to some kind of help," I said.

"Nope. Wouldn't have worked—Lenny got all kinds of help, and all those meds did much more harm than good." Lenny died of intestinal problems. He had many physical ailments, including what was called "simulated

Parkinson's." All of his physical problems were, according to his doctors, attributable to effects of the psychotropic medications he took for several years.

"There are other important things I want to talk about," Lorraine said. "The next is to ask your forgiveness. You could have destroyed me when you found out, but you stuck with Heather and me. You have been caring for both of us—getting me to doctors and stuff like that. That was good of you. Although you do live like a bachelor, sometimes—"

"Thank you," I said.

She continued. "I do want you to know that Ma never forgot that you could not remember who she was that time you met her on the street." Lorraine laughed again.

"I knew who she was—I just couldn't think of her name," I said. It is true that one time I was at the aquarium in Brooklyn with one of my classes when I ran into her and could not recall her name. After I had stammered and stuttered for a few agonizing minutes, trying to introduce her to some of my classroom staff, Fanny stormed off, saying, "I am Fanny Rosenberg, your mother-in-law! Remember me?"

"This is something that you have never let me forget," I said, and laughed. "I will never forget the stricken look on your mother's face."

"I also want to tell you: do not have a funeral service for me. It would be nice to be buried close to Ma, if you can fix that. Just take me and bury me—no service, no rabbi, and nobody but you there. Nobody but you, assuming you want to be at my burial."

"I guess I can do that, but what about Henrietta—she will want to be there, and you should not deny her that chance to mourn you."

"Maybe you are right—well, you can go, Henrietta can go, so maybe could Madeline and Susan. Nobody else. And no rabbi." Madeline is a physical therapist who treated Heather for nearly fifteen years. Susan is one of Lorraine's second cousins. "I don't have a rabbi of my own, for good reason. Do what we did with Ma—just say a prayer and put me in the ground. A simple pine coffin. I know you would want your Pastor Bob to do something, but Christian services are long and boring, and Jewish people—the Jewish people in my family, anyway—will come around only to find out who is in the will."

"Well," I said, "you certainly have hit all the major stereotypes with that statement."

"Let a dying person have her say—the Christians I know want me to be like them, which I ain't, and the Jews I know are too judgmental. That is neither here nor there, now, I guess."

A nurse interrupted the conversation, coming into the room to tell Lorraine she would be taken soon to go do some cardiac tests. Lorraine said she did not want them, but seeing that I was not happy with that response, said she would be ready.

"Did you ever wonder what our lives would have been like if we had never had Heather?" Lorraine asked. Before I could answer, she continued. "Sometimes I have no memory of a life before Heather. Well, she is still here and in good shape, so I guess I—we—did right by her." I did not know if Lorraine had more to say, so I just nodded, "Yes."

"There is one more question I want to ask you," Lorraine said.

"About Heather?" I asked.

"No, I know she will be well taken care of. She was blessed in having you for a father. Actually, come to think of it, there is something about Heather. I hope you will bury her next to me, when her time comes." Lorraine looked at me for a long second and then added, "I am sure you don't want to be buried there, right?"

"First off, if you are buried where your mother and Lenny are buried, I can't be. They take only Jewish dead people," I reminded her. "Plus, as we have discussed, I plan to be cremated. That's okay—we had thirty-three years together. I don't think either one of us would want an eternity. And you know it is already in my will that I should be cremated."

"Jewish people aren't cremated," Lorraine said. "If you are cremated, how can anyone come visit you? Speaking of which, if you do come visit me, I hope you will also stop by and visit Ma and Lenny."

"I could do that—I always did it with you," I said. "Right now I am making no plans to do it, however—I expect you to get better."

"There is really no chance of that," Lorraine said and lowered her head. She recovered quickly and continued. "Do you think you will be going to Colorado? If you do—how can you bury Heather beside me?" I have family in Colorado, and we had discussed moving there for support and help after I retired from teaching.

"Getting Heather back to New York would not be, I think, that much of a problem."

"Do you remember when we had the argument about how long we had been married?"

"That was funny," I said. "The argument was over whether we had been married thirty miserable years, or thirty-one miserable years. I don't remember who was right—" I paused for second and then said, "To change the subject, I want to say Heather is as blessed, maybe more so, in her mother. She also chose her mother well."

"Wow! Hooray! You finally gave me a compliment! I guess the millennium did come after all."

Lorraine reached out and took my hand. "You know, you were also right when you insisted we both find lives besides taking care of Heather. I wasted a lot of time resisting that but did some nice things doing it."

"That's nice," I said. "Thank you for that."

"I suppose I should also apologize for my family."

"Your family—why?"

"Well, you certainly did not hook up with me to be hated by Ma, and you did nothing to deserve it, except for leaving me. But she would have hated you anyway, I guess. She was just a very afraid person and lashed out at everyone." Lorraine smiled. "Now, you going to apologize for your family?"

"Nope—why should I?"

"I am just kidding. Just kidding—why don't we ever see them anymore?"

"I see some of them fairly regularly."

"They see you, they see Heather, but they don't see me."

In one of her depressed periods, Lorraine had accused two of my brothers and their wives of turning me against her because she was Jewish. Rather than remind her of that episode, I said simply, "They wanted to come around, but either you were sick or Heather was. They didn't want to be a bother, I guess."

Lorraine looked doubtful but said, "I guess it did start the first time I got sick. Ah well, all gone and past, now. Nothing to be done, I guess." Lorraine sighed again.

I stood to leave. "I better get gone," I said.

Lorraine did not let go of my hand. "I need to say that I have always loved you. You have reasons to hate me, and I am sorry for them; but I always loved you, and I love you now."

"I love you, too," I said, and embraced her as she sat on the bed. "We will talk more later. I will see you this afternoon."

"I hope so, because it would mean I am alive then," Lorraine said, "but I didn't ask you my last important question."

"Oh?" I said. "What is that?"

"Please tell me," Lorraine said, "that you did not vote for Hillary Clinton to be United States Senator for New York."

I could only laugh and shake my head. "You should leave that poor lady alone." I left and went to my meeting.

I never saw Lorraine alive again. She had a heart attack in the early afternoon, slipped into a coma, and never woke from it. She died on the morning of December 11, 2001. Her burial was not precisely as she asked. First, three of the supervisors from my school showed up because they did not think I should face burying Lorraine alone. I also asked a rabbi to say the prayers.

THIRTY-FOUR

So, there it is. Well, not exactly all.

A word should also be said about the men and women we have known these past years. We have seen ordinary people in extraordinary situations. Not everybody acted in ways that did them credit. Bill Dugan, in spite of the fact that we considered suing him for the error Mark Billings made on the original complaint, did a brilliant and effective job of telling our story in court. He wasn't sued simply because I realized, once I calmed down, that the whole thing was not about Lorraine and me, it was about Heather and getting resources to keep her safe. With Bill's help and the help of Mark Billings, for that matter, we were able to do that.

Bill, I know, was absolutely sincere in saying he wanted to help a little girl who was denied a chance to live her life as most of us do and take for granted. It can be said, of course, that Bill and his firm made a pile of money in the process. The amount he was paid, as far as I am concerned, is fair and just compensation for the work done.

Judge James was an example of the American court system at its very best. He is honest, capable, and compassionate. He has learned, and he could teach many others, that achieving a high station in life does not excuse the achiever from simple, ordinary human considerations. Judge James has a sense of the dignity and worth of all human beings, which he translates into everyday actions. It is imposing and wonderful to witness.

Lorraine had to be one of the most courageous women in the world. She certainly had "issues," as they say in current lingo, but those problems only made her actions more courageous and selfless. What she did, she did from love for Heather. Lorraine was a completely dependent person, but would not give up her child in the face of illness, family opposition, or a swirling, chaotic personal life. In the end, she prevailed: Heather lives at home and will do so as long as I am physically and mentally able to supervise her care.

There are some heavies, too.

Balnick, whose one irresponsible act as a doctor cost him a career, is, I am told, no longer in practice in the United States. I know his New York office was up for sale shortly after the case was closed. It seems the hospital's carrier went after him to collect the amount they paid above the ten percent liability the jury placed on them. The story also got around that he planned to be married the day Lorraine was in labor at the hospital. The bride-to-be, however, ran away, and Balnick spent the day in an angry search for her. He could not, if this story is true, as Bill and Steve said it was, be bothered to tend a patient because of his rage at being dumped.

I have long since forgiven Balnick. Lorraine said she forgave him, too, but the occasional curse and diatribe would slip out in spite of that profession. Part of the sad commentary about this case is that he lost his practice because he could not get malpractice insurance, not because his peers said to him that his conduct was intolerable. As far as I know, nobody in the medical profession said, "Let's check into this man and what he did. Are we sure we want somebody who could do that treating vulnerable people?"

Balnick aside, the true heavies in the long run are the attorneys. Attorneys were the tools of the insurance companies who stalled our case in the hope Heather would die and, thereby, lessen their payout. One attorney actually suggested to the jury that Heather could not be aware of their verdict, so why bother? Attorneys demanded that Balnick go through the humiliation of a trial when they must have understood he did not have a prayer of escaping the judgment of the jury. In all this, they kept us at bay, hurting while caring for our daughter; hurting knowing that she had been done grievous harm.

Not nice people, not decent people.

It is an interesting and curious fact that our help and support in the past years have come from individuals or private institutions. The court and the school are, I suppose, governmental institutions. So, let me say with those two exceptions, any help we got from an agency of the government has been small, demeaning, and grudging. We don't need their help now, but pause for a moment and consider those hundreds of thousands of people with children like Heather who do need help. Maybe I am naïve to be surprised that this society does not offer help to its most helpless without making them struggle and fight for it. This society allows seniors to eat cat food and small children to go hungry and without regular medical care. Is America proud of this? Does America know? Does America care?

While commenting on the society in general, I would like to throw in here another related, but not entirely relevant, item. After Heather's trial, I sat on a jury in a case trying an accused crack cocaine dealer for the murder of another alleged drug dealer. It took the attorneys in Heather's case nearly three days to impanel the six-person jury. The jury of twelve to try a man for murder took less than an hour. I have often wondered why the difference: the only conclusion I could come to is the fact that in our case money was involved, so jury selection was much more careful. Whatever the full reason is, this is another sad commentary on our legal system.

I do want to add that there seems to be more acceptance of the handicapped in the society now. It was always nice and sweet to have strangers or neighbors greet us when we take walks, or are out in public for other reasons. There was a time when most people would simply look away as we walked by, but in the past few years, people we meet respond to Heather in a positive way. Many who know us, greet us with, "Hello, Heather, and hello, Heather's dad." I am also told frequently that I am doing a great thing caring for her, or, as one man told me, "it is a blessing."

I have a friend who is involved with New Age religion. She tells me that everything happens for a reason. I cannot find a reason for what happened to Heather. It will always seem to me to be a tragedy and a waste. But in this whole story there is a message for me. I am, in fact, a restless and tense person. There is, in me, a desire to keep moving, or more accurately, keep running. The message here for me is simply, "Slow down. Wait. Don't run. Your life is here. There is joy and richness here where you are." Without Heather as an anchor, I have no idea where I would be or what I would be doing, or, for that matter, what I would have done with my life.

Heather is forty-one years old now. She is safe and living at home with me in Grand Junction, Colorado. I can rest at night knowing that if my time comes before hers, I have done as much as is humanly possible to keep her from facing the horror of an institution, especially a New York State institution. Perhaps knowing that your child is as safe as you can make her is as much as a parent can hope for. Whatever the future holds for Heather, it is my most profound wish that she somehow knows that she is loved, simply because she *is*. I also hope she knows that I am content holding her spoon as she eats, bathing her, and caring for her. It is a complete joy to hear her laugh and shout in accompaniment to the music I play for her, and to feel her lean against me and see her smile as I read or talk to her. Heather is a reward unto herself. I am blessed to have her, and I pray that she will be well and with me for years to come.